To KIMBERLY BAIRD /

ALL THE BEST TO A

BEAUTIFUL WOMAN!

ENJOY!

William C. Arden

1994

Lady Bluebeard

Lady Bluebeard

The True Story of

Love and Marriage,

Death and Flypaper

William C. Anderson

Fred Pruett Books
2928 Pearl St.
Boulder, CO 80301

To Blake and Brooke Anderson

. . . an unbeatable pair to draw to

Preface

This is a true story.

In the interests of clarity and continuity, some dramatic license has been taken with dialogue, as well as with a few of the peripheral characters.

Endeavoring to make this account as factual as possible, extensive research was made of newspaper, book, and magazine excerpts of the time; trial transcripts and exhibits were obtained; birth and death certificates provided authenticity; interviews were held with the last coherent relative of the accused.

The major characters are all real, the dates are correct, and the incidents happened just as depicted.

Acknowledgements

The author is deeply indebted to the many contributors who have made possible the publication of this book. To name just a few who have cooperated above and beyond the call of duty:

Arthur Hart, Director Emeritus Idaho State Historical Society, a good friend and the prime mover in convincing me that there was a fascinating story in the life of Lyda Southard.
    Linda Parkinson, Twin Falls librarian
    Linda Wright, Clerk of the Court, Twin Falls, Idaho
    Rachel Vanderpool, Court Services, Twin Falls, Idaho
    Jim Munn, sheriff of Twin Falls County, Idaho
    Daniel B. Meehl, Twin Falls County Fifth District judge
    Jerry Woolley, Deputy Clerk Records Manager Fifth
          Judicial District, Twin Falls, Idaho
    Don Waldhalm, Old Idaho Penitentiary historian
    Patricia Byron, Education Specialist, Old Idaho
          Penitentiary
    Elizabeth Jaycox, Idaho Historical Society
    Alan Virta, archivist, Boise State University
    Pamela Wright, Twin Falls Sunset Memorial Park
    June Merrell, Garden City, Idaho, librarian
    Kathy Hodges, Idaho State Historical Society
    Guila Ford, Idaho State Historical Society
    John Yandell, Idaho State Historical Society

And I would like to thank the following writers from whose published works I unabashedly stole pertinent information:

    Rosalie Sorrels, "Way Out in Idaho"
    R. Murphy, "Behind Gray Walls"
    Betty Penson-Ward, "Idaho Women In History"
    Hubert Dail, *True Detective Mysteries*
    Bob Arentz, "Murder In Idaho; a Compilation of Famous
          Idaho Crimes"
    Dick d'Easum, *Idaho Stateman*
    John Corlett, *Idaho Statesman*

A special thanks to Mr. Darrell Sweet of Jerome, Idaho, nephew of Lyda Southard, who was instrumental in adding a hitherto unknown dimension to our lady of mystery.

A doff of the boater to Kirk Mitchell of the *Twin Falls Times News*, whose diligent research and writing skills contributed immensely to this project.

And finally a deep bow to literary representative Jennifer Lyons, editor Merilee Eggleston, and publisher Fred Pruett, whose endeavors to make a silk purse out of a sow's ear proved invaluable.

Lyda Southard's Famous Apple Pie

(Folksong sung to the tune of "Annie Laurie")

Oh, Twin Falls' farms are bonnie
In the middle of July,
And 'twas there that Lyda Southard
Baked her famous apple pie.
Her famous apple pie . . .
Which ne'er forgot will be . . .
And for Lyda's deep dish apple pie
I'd lay me down and dee.

She sprinkled it with cinnamon,
A dash of nutmeg too,
And sugared it with arsenic,
A tasty devil's brew.
That famous apple pie . . .
Which ne'er forgot will be . . .
And for Lyda Southard's apple pie,
Men lay them down to die.

Four times she picked her apples
And put them in a pie.
'Twas just dessert, she murmured,
I never thought they'd die,
I never thought they'd die,
I never thought they'd die,
She was just a country housekeeper
Who never thought they'd die.

Oh Lyda's got her just deserts,
She's in the jailhouse strong,
Her piecrust it was short and sweet,
Her sentence it is long.
Her sentence it is long . . .
Her sentence it is long . . .
Oh, Lyda's in the jailhouse now,
Her sentence it is long.

— *Rosalie Sorrels*

Prologue

Farmer William Trueblood was frustrated by the whimsical and merciless Missouri weather, and fed up with the floods, the heat waves, and the hail. When he saw an inviting flyer in the window of Hiram Jones's Mercantile Store in Keytesville one hot summer day in 1906, the good man's life was changed.

The flyer depicted a rancher in Idaho holding an apple so large it could only have come from the Garden of Eden. "Land for the taking," extolled the circular. "Irrigated water on demand and never-ending sunshine. Come to Twin Falls, Idaho, the land of opportunity."

For the trusting and gullible Trueblood, the flyer was a revelation. That winter he packed his Bible, his tools, his furniture, and his family on a train and headed west. Upon reaching Twin Falls, he secured some fertile ranch land near the river and built a two-story house with a large covered porch for his wife and seven children.

But his fourteen-year-old daughter Lyda was unhappy. She all but refused to talk to her father, whom she thought had let her down. He had sold their Missouri farm and all the animals to pay for their new farm on the Salmon tract. Lyda loved those animals: the pigs whose tails she braided, the cows she had named, and the horses that always greeted her in the barn. William Trueblood was distressed about his usually sparkling, outgoing daughter. He promised Lyda he would replace the animals with ivory dolls and silk dresses.

But this was not to be. The new Salmon Falls Dam, which was to feed the Truebloods' thirsty wheat fields, was a bust. The spring of 1907 filled the dam only a quarter of the way. What little irrigation water there was disappeared into the canal ditches, along with the Truebloods' hopes of a flourishing future. Instead of having new clothes and dolls, Lyda trudged barefooted down the dusty driveway to the main road where a school buggy picked up her and her brothers and sisters and took them to school.

Their fortunes improved only slightly during the ensuing years. Thanks mainly to the assistance of a gentleman named Ira B. Perrine, one of Twin Falls' more distinguished gentlemen, William Trueblood did barely manage to keep his head above water.

Stella Perrine, Ira's daughter, turned out to be Lyda's closest friend. Stella's father saw to it that his children properly reflected his prosperity. Stella always wore lace dresses, a bonnet, white socks, and patent leather shoes. Lyda went through high school in her scuffed shoes and hand-me-downs, all the while imagining herself wearing Stella's clothes and climbing into the nice buggy that took Stella to school every day.

But in spite of the financial gulf between them, the two girls remained fast friends all through their high school years. Lyda loved nothing better than visiting the Perrine's remodeled beehouse called the Brook Lodge on the Blue Lakes Ranch. The house was painted white with green trim, its entrance flanked by two Colorado blue spruce trees. The porch was enclosed and screened; a walkway was built out over the water. Inside, the wood paneled walls were decorated with rattlesnake and bobcat skins, and a woven green grass rug covered the floor. A mahogany phonograph cabinet threw back the rays of electric light bulbs. Lyda truly loved the place.

Shortly after they graduated from the Twin Falls High School, the two girls found themselves relaxing in the clover field on the Blue Lakes Ranch.

Lyda rolled over on her back, laced her hands behind her head, and looked up at the fleecy cotton balls scudding across the sky. "I love it out here," she said.

Stella looked over at her best friend. Then her eyes roamed across the clovered field, stopping at the two saddle horses that were tethered to the large oak tree. "I do too. Our own private getaway place. I'm going to miss it."

"Me too. But I'm not going to miss our ranch."

"I know. I'm sorry your folks have had such a rough time making ends meet. But you have to admit this is a beautiful place. And you love all these ranch animals so."

"I love the animals." She glanced over at her roan grazing in the meadow. "Especially Chester. I'm going to miss him." She reached over to pat the panting dog that had collapsed beside her. "And I'm going to miss Old Tige."

"I never saw anyone as crazy about animals as you are. Personally, I like the two-legged kind."

"So I've noticed."

Stella rolled over, cupped her chin with her hands, and studied the face of her girl friend. "You're a funny girl, Lyda."

"Fiddlesticks. Don't call me funny. Just because I don't like living on a ranch. All my life I've lived on a lonely old ranch. First in Missouri, then here. I'm tired of it."

"Nothing wrong with living on a nice ranch."

"For you, fine. You have a beautiful place. But ours is a pigsty."

"It is not."

"'Tis. Ranching's not for me. I like nice things. Like you have, Stella. Beautiful clothes. And I want to travel to exotic places. Meet interesting people." A fire came into her eyes. "I want to dance till dawn."

"Me too." Stella sighed. "Are you sorry we've graduated from high school?"

"No."

"Why not? According to my folks, high school's supposed to be the best time in our life."

"Oh, it's all right." Lyda plucked a dried dandelion, brought its cluster of seeds close to her face. "But I'm ready for new adventures. I love the lights of the city."

"And handsome boys, Lyda." Stella shot her friend a lascivious look. "I know you."

"Not handsome boys, Stella. Handsome *men*."

"Well, you sure won't have any trouble finding them. Not with that beautiful red hair. And everybody knows you have the cutest figure in school."

"Stella, you're just saying that."

"I am not. Look at me." Stella stuck out her chest. "Two fried eggs. Over easy."

"You have a nice, slim figure."

"Not according to Stan Philpot. He says Sally, his brood sow, has bigger teats than I have."

"You tell Stan Philpot to take a flying leap at the moon."

"Not hardly. He's the only one who'll take me dancing." Stella sighed. "I'd give anything to have breasts like yours. Not to mention your cute behind."

"You're just as cute as I am, Stella. And you wear the prettiest clothes in school."

"Ha! That's a laugh. You have every boy in high school panting after you."

"Oh, pshaw."

"If I didn't know you so well, I might think you lowered your bloomers on special occasions."

Lyda smiled. "You know that's not true. I don't wear any bloomers."

Stella giggled. "I know."

Lyda puckered up and blew the cluster of dried dandelion seeds into the air. As she watched them wafting away on the summer breeze, her face assumed a pensive, faraway look. "No, I'll never give my body away. It's the only thing I have. I'm tired of being poor. Whoever gets it is really going to have to pay for it."

Stella smiled at being a party to this confidence. "I admire you, Lyda. I wish I could say that. This old body of mine, fudge! I'd give it to anyone who'd take it. Gladly."

Lyda turned on her. "Stella Perrine! Don't you talk that way. Don't you *ever* talk that way! Your body is your temple. The Bible says so. So treat it like one."

"That's easy for you to say. You with your gorgeous – "

"I don't want to talk any more about it." Lyda jumped to her feet, started running for her horse. "Come on."

Stella rose, dutifully following. As they leaped onto their horses, she asked, "Where are we going?"

"Down to the river," Lyda slapped her horse with the reins.

"To the river? What for?"

"Don't ask so many dumb questions. We're going skinny dipping."

"Skinny dipping! Hot spit!"

Chapter One

"Val," said the prosecuting attorney, "you must somehow find out if the evidence justifies digging up Ed Meyer's body."

Deputy Sheriff Virgil Ormsby shifted uneasily in his chair, mentally sizing up this young lawyer who was the new prosecuting attorney. He wasn't sure he was going to like Frank Stephan. "Yes, sir." He looked over at his boss, the third man in the room.

Sheriff E. R. Sherman was a stern, sober individual with a mane of white hair and bushy black eyebrows that shaded deep-set eyes. He wore his mantle of authority with a certain down-home dignity. He had also just been elected to his new job in the January 1921 election, and he was eager to make a good impression in front of the prosecuting attorney, "It's up to us to get to the bottom of the Meyer mystery if we possibly can."

Ormsby scratched his long nose. So the damned Meyer case had resurfaced. Well, at least it was better than spending his time trying to convince old Cecil Jones to keep his cows out of Jeremy Johnston's cornfield. That damned blunderbuss Johnston carried around was going to blow up one of these days and hurt somebody. Ormsby crossed his legs as he listened to the slightly nasal voice of his boss.

"Val, I'm delegating you to work on this case. As you know, it's a real can of worms. You're going to have to backtrack to the time of Meyer's death. Go out to the Blue Lakes Ranch. Talk to the boys out there. Some of them are responsible for the rumors that Ed Meyer was murdered."

"Right, Sheriff."

"Find out if Meyer had any enemies. Get all the details about his marriage. I hate to do it to old Ed, but we'll dig him up if the facts warrant."

"We're in the spotlight, Val," said the prosecuting attorney. "The sheriff and I were elected because we promised to clear this matter up. Don't get any preconceived ideas about anyone's guilt, but let's just see where the evidence will take us."

"Yes, sir."

"And remember," added the lawyer, "keep this under wraps. Mention the case only to those people who can provide information. Then swear them to secrecy. If a murder has been committed, and we're to solve it, we'll get much farther working under cover."

"I agree, gentlemen." Ormsby uncrossed his legs and picked up his hat. "Will that be all?"

"That's pretty much it, Val," said the sheriff. "Good luck."

Ormsby rose, moistened his lower lip with his tongue. "I'll do my best." He put on his hat and went out the door.

The prosecuting attorney leaned back in his chair, laced his fingers behind his head, and looked over at the sheriff. "Well, Sherman, what do you think?"

Sherman met the lawyer's eyes. "I'll admit Val Ormsby doesn't present a real striking figure. But he's got two things going for him. One, he knows Twin Falls, Idaho, and its people like the back of his hand. And two, the man has a native intelligence and the tenacity of a bulldog. I have a gut feeling that if anyone can get to the bottom of this thing, Val Ormsby can."

"Let's just hope you're right. For the sake of both our new careers . Let's just hope you're right."

Deputy Sheriff Ormsby turned up his coat collar to deflect the biting winter wind as he headed for his car. Pulling out of the diagonal parking space in front of the courthouse, he soon passed the Grille Cafe, and his mind whirred back to his old friend, Ed Meyer.

It was here at the Grille Cafe that Ed had first met the pretty young widow who had waited on his table. Lyda McHaffie had literally swept the big, bashful German-American off his feet with her pretty red hair and petite figure. Lyda had become Ed's wife only a few short months ago, and it didn't seem possible that Ed had now taken up residence in the Twin Falls cemetery.

As Ormsby left town and picked up speed toward the Blue Lakes Ranch, his thoughts turned to Lyda. He had known her since she was a very pretty child with hair in braids that cascaded down her back. She had been one of seven Trueblood children, and possibly the favorite.

Ormsby remembered when the slim, pretty girl had first married a young man by the name of Robert Dooley. Dooley hailed from Missouri, and they had gone off to live on a ranch there in perpetual bliss when Dooley suddenly up and died. To ameliorate her grief, Lyda returned to Twin Falls. Not long after, she became enamored of a cafe owner, Billy McHaffie, and married him.

Everyone in Twin Falls knew Billy and Lyda, and they all hoped Lyda would find peace and happiness in her second marriage. But this was not to be. McHaffie caught the flu during the epidemic, and in spite of being a very hale and healthy individual, died unexpectedly.

And now poor Lyda's string of bad luck had continued with her marriage to Ed Meyer, a likable young buck who had been struck down in the shank of life.

Three marriages, thought Ormsby. Quite a number for a pretty girl only twenty-seven years of age. And gregarious Ed Meyer, who could lift a brewery horse, died barely a month after his marriage to Lyda. It was no wonder the citizens of Twin Falls were stunned. And it was only natural that rumors began to circulate that Meyer might have been poisoned by some enemy.

Dr. J. F. Coughlin, who attended Meyer during his sickness, had stated that his patient had died of ptomaine poisoning. But his associate, Dr. Hal Bieler, pathologist and chemist, was of the opinion Meyer had suffered from typhoid fever. Because of the difference of opinion held by the experts, an autopsy was ordered.

The Twin Falls citizenry waited tensely as Ed Meyer's remains were studied. Would the postmortem show typhoid — or some other hideous malady? Could it be possible that some poison or dangerous foreign element might appear in Ed Meyer's body? The autopsy showed traces of typhoid germs in Meyer's remains. Hal Bieler was jubilant that his theory had proved correct.

However, Dr. Coughlin was only partially convinced of the accuracy of Dr. Bieler's diagnosis. He had never known a case of typhoid that was not accompanied by high fever. And Ed Meyer had shown only a slight fever right up to the time of his demise.

The results of the autopsy did temporarily silence the reports that Meyer had been poisoned by enemies unknown, and the winsome Lyda's husband was buried in the little Twin Falls cemetery. But although Ed Meyer was finally laid to rest, rumors of foul play concerning his demise were not. No one seemed to know where the rumors came from, but a lot of them seemed to be circulating around the ranch where Ed Meyer had been the foreman.

The road turned off from the dry plateau and into the Snake River gorge. As Ormsby slowed his car, he thought of the conversation that had been reported to him by Louise Hoodenpyle, Ed's sister, shortly after Ed's death. She had been present when Mr. Trueblood had visited his daughter.

"Lyda," her father had said, "there's talk of digging up Ed's body and examining it again. What do think?"

"That's a good idea," Lyda had responded, her lips drawn into a tight line. "I'd like to see it done." Then she had turned to Ed's sister. "I suppose you know that Ed left some land, some money, and a little insurance. I want you to know that I don't need it and don't want it. I want it to be divided between you and my father."

Ormsby mulled this as he saw the tops of the Lombardy poplars that marked the outskirts of the ranch loom up ahead. If there were any foul play connected with the untimely death of Ed Meyer, it certainly could not have been conceived by that pretty little redhead who had been at his side when he died. Yet, the rumors persisted. And as with most rumors, it was very difficult to remove fact from fiction. Some of the locals believed Ed had been poisoned from eating unwashed fruit that had been sprayed with insecticides. Others thought someone might have been jealous of his marriage to the pretty waitress, and had slipped something into his home brew.

There had even been those who had expressed suspicion of his new bride, who obviously had never known her. Lyda herself could have easily dispelled these suspicions if she had only consented to a press conference with the local newspapers. But she had left town shortly after the funeral, and no one seemed to know of her whereabouts. Discovering the reason for this untimely disappearance would certainly be the first order of business on the agenda of Ormsby's new assignment.

Chapter Two

As one of Twin Falls' most illustrious entrepreneurs, Ira B. Perrine listed the beautiful Blue Lakes Ranch as his favorite project. He had used the greenhouse effects of the Snake River Canyon and its rich soil to grow an orchard of softball-sized peaches and five varieties of apples. Perrine built a beehouse on the edge of Alpheus Creek and filled it with a hundred bee stands. The bees pollinated his thousands of fruit trees, and he had a thriving business selling the honey at market.

But Perriene was not satisfied with the proceeds of his productive Blue Lakes Ranch. He knew he could multiply his profits by luring an army of farmers to the area. He persuaded bankers from Chicago to finance the construction of the American Falls Dam and the Salmon Falls Dam to lure farmers into south central Idaho. He was convinced that he could turn the seas of aqua-colored sagebrush into golden waves of wheat by introducing water onto the prairie through a canal system.

In the winter of 1907, posters on bank and store windows in the Midwest had lured droves of farmers from the wheat and cornfields to the sage-covered plots of land in Idaho. One of these circulars, depicting Edward Meyer, foreman of the Blue Lakes Ranch, holding a cantaloupe-sized apple, had lured William Trueblood to Idaho. But when the canal company owned largely by Perrine didn't deliver water from the boon-doggle Salmon Falls Dam, many of the transplanted farmers lost their shirts. Their children, like Lyda and her siblings, also wore tattered clothes and were lucky to have a full lunch pail to take to school.

But none of these crashed dreams were evident at the beautiful Blue Lakes Ranch. It had plenty of water and, under the stewardship of its industrious German foreman, had become a picture postcard working ranch.

Ira Perrine spent little time at his ranch, his presence being demanded by his many entrepreneurial projects elsewhere, and his wife preferred to live in the newly renovated beehouse across the river. As a result, the day-to-day operation of the farm was pretty much left up to the capable and likable Ed Meyer. That is, until his unexpected demise.

Turning into the driveway, Ormsby's touring car growled up to the white ranch house with the black smoke issuing from its chimney. He brought his car to a halt, paused with his hand on the car door handle while a veil of dust settled, then alit and walked over to the back door. He knocked sharply.

The door was thrown open by a large man in blue denim overalls. The pantlegs were pushed down into boot tops, and a brown flannel shirt open at the top exposed a large Adam's apple that bobbed as the big man spoke. "Yeah?"

"Name's Val Ormsby," said the deputy sheriff, trying to place the strange face that met him at the door. "I'm the deputy sheriff of Twin Falls County. Mind if I come in?"

"Whadda ya want?" asked the big man, blocking the door.

"I'd like to ask you boys out here on the ranch a few questions."

"About what?"

"About Ed Meyer."

"Ed Meyer ain't here. He's dead."

"Yes. I know. That's what I want to talk to you about."

The big man stared at Ormsby for a moment, sizing up the visitor. Then he stood away from the door. "Come on in."

"Thank you." The deputy stepped into a big room where a fire was roaring in an open fireplace. Ormsby's eyes grappled with the winter twilight that filtered feebly into the room, making out the figures of two other men facing the fireplace. Ormsby tried to recognize the faces that were staring at him intently.

"This here's Val Ormsby," said the big man, motioning the deputy to a chair. "From the sheriff's office."

Suddenly one of the men stood up, and Ormsby recognized Bud Taylor. Taylor had been one of Meyer's closest friends on the ranch. "What brings you here, Val?" asked Taylor, pulling up another chair.

Ormsby took the proferred chair, and Taylor resumed his seat as the deputy explained his mission. When he had finished, he said, "I want you to tell me just what happened before Meyer's death. Anything that might have any bearing at all on this case."

"All right," said Taylor. "We'll tell you everything we know. And

I'm glad our new sheriff's doing something about old Ed Meyer. You ask me, there's something rotten in Denmark."

"I am asking you, Bud. Let's have it."

Taylor leaned back in his chair and crossed his arms. "Well, to begin at the beginning, Ed went into Twin Falls one day and Lyda McHaffie, as she was known then, waited on him at the Grille Cafe. He fell for her like a ton of bricks. Next thing I knew, Ed told me he had been secretly married. You coulda knocked me over with a feather. I just couldn't understand this, because Ed had never paid much attention to women. Too bashful. And I didn't understand why Ed got married secretly. We could have had a real shivaree. Everyone liked that big German. So why have a secret wedding?"

"Go on," said Ormsby, taking out a note pad and moistening a pencil with his tongue. "Don't leave anything out."

"Well, he married Lyda and they spent one night together at a hotel in Twin Falls. The next day Ed came back here to the ranch, and Lyda stayed on at the hotel. He had gotten the impression that his new wife was quite well to do, and owned a big ranch up in Montana. I guess she did. Way Ed talked, they were planning on pooling their financial interests. Wouldn't have taken Ed long, cause he didn't have a pot to piss in.

"Anyway, he told me what a swell businesswoman she was and how she had insisted on his taking out a life insurance policy as soon as they were married. Ed said he would soon be leaving Idaho to take her to Montana where he would look after her land investments. Although they were married early in August, we didn't see Lyda around here until the latter part of the month. That's when she came out to see Ed, and stayed all night. Course, their marriage was no secret after that."

"Do you remember the exact date?" asked Ormsby.

Taylor searched the ceiling as if expecting to find the date hidden in the floral wallpaper. "I think she arrived on Tuesday, the twenty-sixth of August. I remember, because the next day it was hotter'n blazes, and after the noon meal Ed and Ben Squires were taken sick. Squires was pretty bad, but Ed was worse. We heard Ed was getting better, and then suddenly we got the news that he had up and died. Squires, of course, got well."

"Squires?" said Ormsby. "I don't believe I know him. Any idea where I might find this Ben Squires?"

"Pretty good idea," said Taylor, pointing. "He's sitting over there in the corner."

Ormsby turned to stare intently at a medium-sized man all but obscured in the flickering firelight. "You're Ben Squires?"

"So I'm told. Glad to meet ya, Sheriff."

Ormsby rose and crossed the room to shake hands. "Pleasure's mine. What can you add to Bud's account?"

Squires took Ormsby's hand, but remained seated, teetering on the back legs of his chair. "Not a hell of a lot."

"Have you any idea what made you sick?"

"Can't say as I have. Lyda said afterward that it might have been string beans that poisoned us. I thought that kind of odd at the time, 'cause we didn't have string beans that day."

"Did you and Meyer eat at the same table?"

"Yep. And he didn't seem to be any sicker than I was at first. But he got worse. On the Sunday following the day he was taken sick, Lyda came over to where I was sleeping in a tent over by the barn. She said the doctors were doing all they could, but she didn't think Ed would pull through."

Ormsby scanned the faces in the firelight. "Do you know if there was any poison brought into the house before Ed died? Any kind of insecticide . . . rat poison?"

As Ormsby nailed each of the men with his questioning look, one by one they shook their heads. "Not that we know of," said Bud Taylor. "Nothing."

"Okay, gents. Anything else you can think of?"

Taylor shrugged. "I guess that's about it. Lyda came back to the ranch for a couple of hours after the funeral. She went over her late husband's belongings, picked up some papers, then got into her blue touring car and took off down the road. She barely took time to say goodbye. Haven't seen her since."

Ormsby closed his notebook and tucked it into his shirt pocket. He rose, put on his hat, and thanked the men for their time. As he reached the door, he turned back. "If anything comes up that might shed some light on this case, I can be reached at the sheriff's office. I'd appreciate a call."

Bud Taylor escorted him to the door and let him out. As Ormsby hunched into the cold wind, he could barely hear Taylor's words, all but drowned in the winter's fury. "We find out anything, Val, you'll be the first to know. As I told you, something's mighty fishy about ole Ed's death."

Darkness now joined the howling wind as Ormsby drove his car back to Twin Falls. Deep in thought, he squinted at the beams of light picking up the road that threaded through the Snake River Gorge. There seemed to be something almost ominous about the men he had just met with in the ranch house. Did they know more than they were telling? Could any one of them have had something to do with Meyer's death?

At this point Ormsby had more questions than answers. On the morrow he would redouble his efforts to locate Lyda Meyer. She would be easy to track down. And if anyone knew the answers, she certainly should. In the meantime, there was one man who might fill in some of the blanks.

He would make an early appointment with Dr. J. F. Coughlin, one of the last people to see Ed Meyer before he died.

Deputy Sheriff Ormsby looked across the office at Dr. Coughlin's white-bearded face. As Ormsby looked deep into the kindly eyes, he was reminded of the Santa Claus on the cover of a recent *Saturday Evening Post* magazine painted by some new up-and-coming artist named Norman Rockwell. "As you know, Doctor, we're investigating the circumstances of Ed Meyer's death. Would you mind telling me about his last hours?"

Dr. Coughlin produced a pipe, picked up a reamer, and started carving out the carbonized tobacco. "Well, Deputy, there's not an awful lot to tell." He tapped the pipe into a wastebasket under his desk. "As you know, Ed Meyer was a rugged sort. Sunburned and muscular from his duties at the ranch. Wasn't a very likely candidate for the ailment that caused his demise."

"So I understand."

The doctor took a pinch of tobacco out of a Prince Albert can and tamped it into the bowl of his pipe. "As I recall, the day Ed Meyer died, his wife, Lyda, was at his bedside. She was holding his hand when suddenly she jumped up and darted out of the room. In the hospital corridor she ran around wildly, until she located a nurse." He lit a kitchen match to the pipe's bowl and began puffing. "This was all told to me later by Nurse Johnson."

"Go on, Doctor."

"Lyda kept running around yelling, 'Ed's dying! Ed's dying! I can see it in his face.' Nurse Johnson tried reassuring the young lady, calming her down. But when the nurse entered the room and saw the condition of the patient, she came running for me. When I arrived at his bedside, Ed was aspirating wildly — "

"Layman's terms, please, Doc," interrupted Ormsby.

"Sorry. Ed Meyer was fighting for air. His face a chalky white. Out of the corner of my eye I could see Lyda standing in the corner of the room, her hands clenched into small fists. Her eyes seemed to be fixed on her husband's face with an almost hypnotic intensity. She seemed to be trying to hold him to life by the power of her desire."

"That hardly describes a woman who might have wanted her husband dead."

Coughlin looked at the lawman curiously. "Indeed, I should think not."

"Go on, Doc."

"Well, that's about it. In spite of our best efforts, Ed Meyer slipped away. His harsh breathing subsided, his body suddenly stiffened, and he died. When it was finally apparent that it was all over, I remember looking at the pretty young lady huddled in the corner. Her eyes met mine, then they glazed over, she let out a little groan and crumpled to the floor. It was several moments before Nurse Johnson and I could revive her."

Ormsby mulled this as he watched the smoke from the doctor's pipe curl toward the ceiling. Then, "That's it?"

"Just about. When we brought Lyda around, she looked up at me, her eyes brimming with tears. She said something like, 'It's just a month today since we were married. What killed him? What could have caused my husband's death?' I told her I didn't really know. That the exact cause would have to be determined by an autopsy. I did say it looked to me like ptomaine poisoning. At this, she looked at me real wild-eyed. 'Poison!' she shrieked. 'How could that be?'

"I quickly tried to reassure her. 'Probably something he ate,' I said, trying to pacify her. Something that had somehow naturally gotten into his system. Then Lyda nodded. Her eyes were still dazed. But she pulled herself together, left the room, and hurried through the corridor and out the door." The doctor took a deep breath. "That's the last time I saw her."

Deputy Sheriff Ormsby shifted gears as he headed up the slight incline of the road that led toward the cemetery. The motion was strictly reflex, as Ormsby's thoughts were a mile away. He couldn't help but dwell on the actions of Lyda at the time of her husband's death. As Doc Coughlin had described it, were these the actions of someone who had just murdered another human being?

He had to be fair. The prosecuting attorney had warned him about making biased decisions. It's true that the finger of suspicion had pointed to Lyda in several ways. Yet, the suspicions were vague, and there was nothing tangible to get a handle on. Might Meyer have been murdered, if indeed he was, by some party or parties outside the range of his friends' suspicions? By someone who had a real motive for getting the ranch foreman out of the way?

Then, as they always did, his thoughts returned to the pretty redhead who seemed to be declared guilty without any kind of trial. If only she were here, she could undoubtedly throw some light on this mystery. But so far, all of his attempts to track her down had led to a brick wall. Where in hell was Lyda, and why had she disappeared so abruptly? Could it be possible that whoever had snuffed out Ed Meyer's life could also have killed Lyda?

Shuddering at the thought, his musings were interrupted by the forbidding sight of the cemetery looming up in the dark. He wasn't exactly sure why he was now finding himself at the graveyard where Ed Meyer was buried, but he was going to leave no stone unturned. Even if it meant old Ed's headstone.

He stopped at the fresh mound of earth that was now the residence of his friend. He took off his hat and stood silently for a moment, braced against the chill wind. Thoughts tumbled through his mind. What secrets were in that big body that lay six feet under the frozen earth? If they were to disinter Ed Meyer, would they find more than just the typhoid germs that had been blamed for his demise?

Shivering, Ormsby got back into his open car and drove until his headlights picked up the cemetery sexton's house. Noting with satisfaction that there was a light in the window, the deputy pulled up in front of the door and stopped. He stepped out of the car, his shoes squeaking as they crunched the frozen snow lining the path that led to the sexton's small house. He knocked on the door.

Sexton Louis Snyder was an elderly, gaunt man who looked as if he might have just emerged from one of the many eternal resting places he attended. A look of surprise crossed his wrinkled face as he opened the door to the shivering deputy sheriff. "Why, if it ain't Val Ormsby."

"Good evening, Louis," Ormsby stomped the snow from his feet and stepped into the small room.

"What brings you out here on a night like this, Sheriff? Colder'n a marble-cutter's hind end."

"Just happened to be in the neighborhood," said Ormsby, shaking snow from his hat. "I'd like to ask you a couple of questions."

"You bet, Val. Would you like to join me in a little toddy? Was just fixing a spot of grog to ward off the night's chill."

"That would be fine." As Ormsby took a chair in front of the grate fire, he held his hands out to the warmth. He watched as the elderly man removed a poker from the fire and plunged it into a large flagon he held in his hand. There was a loud hiss, and then the heady smell of hot buttered rum filled the room. "Nobody makes a hot grog better than you do, Louis."

"That's cause I been at it a long time." He poured the contents of the flagon into two cups and handed one to the deputy. "A mighty long time."

Ormsby took a sip, felt the warmth tingle right down to his toes. "You remember Ed Meyer's funeral?"

"Ed Meyer's?" Did Ormsby detect a hint of a smile on the old sexton's face at the question? "Of course. It was a big funeral. The mourners really muddied up the place."

"Did you notice anything out of the ordinary? Anything at all suspicious?"

The old man took a large gulp of his drink. "Funny you should ask that."

"Funny? Why?"

The sexton suddenly thrust his face forward and peered into the deputy's eyes. "I'll tell you something. It's my job to stay at the grave until the last clod of earth is thrown in. At Ed Meyer's funeral I watched all the mourners leave after the services, all but that pretty widow dressed in black. Then I saw something that really clabbered my buttermilk."

Ormsby paused, his cup halfway to his mouth. "What was that, Louis?"

"I saw," the old sexton's voice became a hoarse whisper, "that the young woman lingered. She stayed until all the others were well out of sight. Then she did the damnest thing." Snyder paused to take another sip of grog.

"For God's sake, man. Out with it."

"Well," the sexton wiped his lips, obviously enjoying the suspense. "After the other mourners had gone, the lady in black stared at the grave for a spell, and finally she lifted her long black veil. And then I saw the expression on her face. You know what?"

"For Christ's sake, what?"

"It was almost like she was in a trance. And then, as God is my witness," Snyder lifted his right, "I heard her laugh."

"You heard her . . . *laugh*?"

The old Sexton's head nodded vigorously. "Laugh! I actually heard her laugh." He shook his right hand. "As God is my witness!"

Chapter Three

A few days later Val Ormsby entered the office of his chief. Sheriff Sherman finished signing several papers on his desk, then tossed them into the out-basket. He turned his full attention to his deputy, as Ormsby took a seat. "So how's it going?" he asked.

The deputy shook his head. "It's pretty rocky, Sheriff. I seem to be swimming upstream. Not making a hell of a lot of progress."

"Bring me up to date, Val."

"Well, it seems a lot of people want to place the responsibility of Ed Meyer's death on his widow. But so far there is no evidence to prove it. I've made several trips out to Blue Lakes Ranch, talked to everyone, gone over the place with a fine-toothed comb. There's no evidence that poison of any kind was in the ranch house before or after the time of Meyer's death. I've checked the stores around here, and no poison was bought by anyone who might have had access to Ed Meyer or the ranch house."

"What did you pick up from the boys at the ranch?"

"Suspicion, mostly. But no evidence. They seem hostile toward Lyda, because she didn't seem to do much grieving over Meyer's death. I guess they have a point. I talked to old Louis Snyder at the cemetery. He even claims Lyda laughed at the funeral. Can you tie that? And someone heard her reply when asked for her permission for the autopsy, 'The doctors can cut Ed up into little pieces as far as I'm concerned.' "

"Very interesting." Sherman took a can of Copenhagen snuff out of his pocket. "We seem to be dealing with a very interesting young lady. But I'm afraid we have to take all this with a grain of salt. These reports may be true, or they may be hearsay."

"Lyda did a couple of things that did arouse suspicion. First, she had put in a claim to collect Ed's insurance after his death, but the insurance company balked on paying it until after the autopsy. Then, after the postmortem, she suddenly abandoned further attempts to collect."

"Now she's dropped out of sight." Sherman introduced a pinch of snuff to his lower lip. "Did anyone see her leave town?"

"No leads so far. She might as well have fallen off the face of this planet. Her mysterious disappearance may account for her failure to go after the twelve thousand dollars of insurance money that was payable after the autopsy was performed." Ormsby flicked a fly off the brim of the hat resting in his lap. "On the other hand, maybe we're coming down too hard on the woman. Suppose Ed Meyer was murdered by some enemy. Lyda may have been wiped out by the same killer. That killer may be someone lurking in the background, whom we've completely ignored."

"That's a possibility. But I rather doubt it." Sherman reached out his foot and pulled an old cuspidor closer to his chair. He directed a volley of tobacco juice into it. "I still can't see why the marriage of those two unlikely candidates ever took place. Why would Ed Meyer buy the cow when he could probably get the milk for free? Let's face it. Lyda did not have the town's most savory reputation."

Ormsby shook his head. "Let's not forget the fact that Ed Meyer was not exactly God's gift to womanhood. As likable as the guy was, John Barrymore he wasn't. Lyda may have been a bit loose, but she was attractive. The young swains in this town buzzed around her like flies on a cowpie. She could have had her pick. So why did she pick that homely, raw-boned, gangly German? I agree with you, Sheriff. The fact that the marriage took place is one of the biggest mysteries of this case."

"And why was the marriage kept secret? Any why did the new bride live apart from Meyer, only going out to the ranch for one brief visit? That's no way for newlyweds to act." Sherman shook his large head slowly. "It just doesn't add up."

"Nope," said Ormsby, "it doesn't. But if I can stay on the case a while longer, Sheriff, I promise to come up with some of the answers."

The sheriff released another volley, wiped his chin, and looked over at his deputy. "Okay, Val. But the prosecuting attorney is tightening the screws. And with you devoting all of your time to this case, our workload is really piling up. I'm afraid if we don't come up with some concrete evidence soon, I'll have to take you off the case."

"You can't do that, Sheriff."

"Oh?" The sheriff gave his deputy an odd look. "And just why can't I?"

"Because I've got a plan. One that just might work."

"You're going to concentrate on finding Lyda?"

"Yes, but not exclusively. I talked to Lyda's father. Old man Trueblood. He's very upset about her disappearance. He thinks something sinister has happened to her, and that she might even be dead. He heard a rumor that she had gone to California. He went out there, but found no trace of her."

"In that case maybe you'd better track her down."

"In due time, Sheriff. But right now I think I have a better plan." Ormsby leaned forward, studying the face of his boss. "I want to backtrack over Lyda's life. Find the people she knew since her first marriage. Find out for sure how her two previous husbands died."

"My God! You think there might be a connection?"

"Not yet." Ormsby flashed a palm. "I don't want any preconceptions. But I want to find out everything there is to know about Lyda's past. Somewhere in that past we'll find a murderer . . . if there is one. I'm positive of it. The facts of her past will tell us whether we should exhume Ed Meyer's body. And these clues just might show us where Lyda is now . . . dead or alive."

The sheriff twanged his cuspidor again. "I can't get too excited about that approach. But maybe it's as good as any. When do you plan to start?"

"I've already started. Thanks to the telephone. If you'll bear with me, I hope to have a full report for you and the prosecuting attorney early next week."

"Okay. You have another week to come up with some hard evidence, Val. Or I'm afraid we're going to have to put this thing in the File-and-Forget drawer."

"Thanks, Sheriff. I won't let you down."

Nellie Ormsby sat up in bed and pulled her nightgown on over her head. As she buttoned it up, she turned to her husband. "I must admit, love, that was not your usual inspired performance."

"Nellie," said Ormsby, rolling over on his back, "I'll thank you to keep a civil foot in your mouth."

"I'm sorry. It's just that you didn't have your usual heart and soul in it." She giggled. "And other things, I might add."

"My God, I've married a fishwife. Watch your tongue, woman. I knew this would happen when Congress passed the amendment allowing females to vote. It's gone to your head."

"And high time." She lay down beside her husband and snuggled up. "I love you, Deputy Sheriff Virgil H. Ormsby. Even though your equipment may, at times, malfunction."

He reached over and patted her. "I'm sorry, Nellie. I guess I've got too many things on my mind."

"It's that Lyda Meyer case, isn't it?"

He sighed. "The damned thing is really bugging me. I've got to get to the bottom of it. And fast. The sheriff has given me an ultimatum. I've got to produce some hard evidence, or he's going to close the case. And I'll never rest until I know whether or not Lyda Meyer is a murderer."

"Well, love, if anyone can get to the bottom of it, you can."

"Thanks for your vote of confidence. I do think my new approach is working out."

"I certainly hope so." He found her lips invading his ear as she muttered huskily, "I'm getting tired of sharing my husband with a sexy redhead."

Deputy Ormsby had not looked forward to this meeting with the sheriff and the prosecuting attorney. He had to make a sales pitch, and he wasn't a very good salesman. It was his job to convince the two men that the Lyda case should not be closed. Not yet, anyway. He squirmed in his chair as the two men waited expectantly for his report. He pulled a notebook from his coat pocket, crossed his legs, cleared his throat, and addressed the prosecuting attorney.

"Sir, Sheriff Sherman has been kind enough to allow me to pursue a somewhat unusual approach to the Lyda Meyer case. For the last week I have been busy compiling a dossier on our Miss Lyda. It's been my contention that if we arm ourselves with the background facts of our fugitive, it may not only help us find her, but may point out the extent of her crimes, if any. To this end," Ormsby glanced at the sheriff, "I'm afraid I've run up quite a phone bill for the county."

Sheriff Sherman reached for his snuff box. "We'll handle that. Important thing is, what have you found out?"

Ormsby leaned forward in his chair. "My digging has really produced some high grade ore. First, I had to find out about Lyda's first marriage to Bob Dooley. I knew the facts in a general way, but I needed more details. The known facts are that Lyda Trueblood married Bob Dooley here in Twin Falls the seventeenth of March, nineteen twelve. Evidently she had known Dooley since they were children together back in Keytesville, Missouri. Lyda's father came from Missouri to Twin Falls when Lyda was a youngster."

Ormsby was gratified to see that the prosecuting attorney was following him closely. "After Lyda and Bob Dooley's wedding, they returned to Keytesville, got some land there, but couldn't make a go of it. They came back here and bought a ranch not far from Twin Falls, with financial help from old man Trueblood. Bob Dooley's brother, Ed, came with them.

"Lyda and the two Dooley brothers seemed to be living happily together on the ranch, and along about nineteen fourteen, Lyda had a baby girl. In August of the following year, Bob Dooley's brother Ed suddenly died. Ed passed away right here in the Twin Falls hospital. Now get this, gentlemen. The hospital records attribute Ed's death to ptomaine poisoning. There was no postmortem."

The prosecuting attorney's brows furrowed. "The hell you say!"

"And listen to this. Bob and Lyda took Ed's body back to Keytesville for burial, and then came back here to their ranch. But only a month later, Bob was taken sick and died. The records are a little vague on this point, but as closely as I can determine, Bob apparently died of typhoid fever. At any rate, Lyda took her husband's body back to Keytesville, and Bob was buried beside his brother."

"Our Lyda," said the sheriff, "was a busy little bee."

Ormsby nodded. "She was. But it gets even better. I've looked up the insurance records, and found that Ed Dooley, the brother-in-law, was insured for two thousand dollars when he died. The policy was payable jointly to Bob Dooley and Lyda. They collected the money, and Lyda, like the dutiful daughter she was, took her thousand and repaid her father for the loan he had advanced to purchase the ranch."

Sherman grunted. "Well now. Our Miss Lyda isn't all bad."

"Here's the topper. Right after Ed's death, Bob Dooley and Lyda took out a joint insurance policy payable to the survivor for twenty-five hundred dollars. When Bob died, Lyda received the money and the ranch property."

The prosecuting attorney shook his head in disbelief. "So that was her game plan. I get the feeling we might be getting hip deep in sheep dip."

Sheriff Sherman slapped his leg with the palm of his hand, nearly spilling his snuff box. "I think your diligence might be paying off, Val. I think this justifies a trip to Missouri. And a talk with the Dooley family."

"I was hoping you'd say that, sir." Warming to the subject, Ormsby continued. "But there's more. We come to Lyda's marriage to William G. McHaffie. I've got to do more checking on this, too. But it appears they were married in May nineteen seventeen, here in Twin Falls. And Lyda's baby girl, then about three years old, died shortly after. Then Lyda and McHaffie moved up by Hardin, Montana, and homesteaded a big piece of land. Apparently things went well. Then in the following year, McHaffie was suddenly stricken with the flu. He died on the twenty-second of October, nineteen eighteen."

Ormsby folded up the notes he had been referring to, and stuck them into his pocket. "So that, gentlemen, is where we stand. I hope you agree with me that we should continue investigating this case."

Sheriff Sherman worked the pinch of snuff around in his lower lip, then planted his eyes on his deputy. "You got my vote, Val. The deaths of these men may have come from natural causes. But if we're going to be suspicious of Ed Meyer's death, we can't ignore these others."

Prosecuting Attorney Stephan rose from his desk, crossed over to the window. He looked down at the lights blinking in the snowy scene below. Then he turned back to the two men and said in measured tones, "That's good work, Val. By all means continue your investigation. Either you're going to chalk up an awful lot to coincidence, or you're going to unearth the biggest crime wave ever to hit this state. Press on, man."

It was a short drive to the small ranch house that had been formerly occupied by Lyda, her then-husband Bob Dooley, and his brother, Ed. Val Ormsby's car labored through several snowdrifts as it pulled up to the little unpainted, pointed-roof house that stood out stark and desolate in the surrounding white-frosted fields. The county records had indicated that the ranch was now owned by Lillian and Jerome Johnson.

Responding to Ormsby's knock on the door, a young woman appeared, wiping her floury hands on her apron. The deputy introduced himself to the pleasant young lady who admitted to being Lillian Johnson. Ormsby took a proferred chair in the front parlor and gladly accepted the offer of a cup of hot chocolate. While it was being prepared, he looked around the small room, mentally visualizing its occupation by the mysterious Dooley distaff. There seemed to be nothing to distinguish it from any other small farmhouse in the area.

As he rested the cup of hot chocolate on his knee and sampled the oatmeal cookies that had accompanied the saucer, he smacked his lips and launched into a brief explanation of his visit. As the young lady's eyes widened, she was asked if she or her husband had ever noted anything suspicious in or about the farmhouse they had purchased.

"We bought the place and moved in shortly after Robert Dooley died," she said, her eyes glistening. "We had heard from the neighbors that the death of the two Dooley boys had been considered strange. You know, being so close together and all." She squeezed her eyes in thought. "Oh yes, and some of the neighbors thought Lyda Dooley hadn't shown any grief when the two men died . . . almost as if she'd expected them to die. One neighbor told my husband that Lyda had really hated Ed Dooley, her brother-in-law, and that Lyda and Ed had quarreled constantly before his death."

Ormsby's eyes narrowed. "Good cookies, Mrs. Johnson."

"Thank you, sir."

"When you moved in, did you find any evidence of poison? Poison of any kind?"

She shook her head slowly. "No. Not that I can remember."

"You looked the place over carefully?"

"Oh, yes. The place was a mess. I don't think Lyda was much of a housekeeper. We had the whole place thoroughly cleaned, and the water tested. Robert Dooley had died of typhoid, you know. I wanted to make sure our water was not contaminated. But the water was all right."

Ormsby rose and put his saucer on the fireplace mantel. "Do you mind if I look around the place? Especially in the basement and the barn?"

"Why, no." Lillian Johnson was certainly going to have something to tell her whist club. "Not at all."

Ormsby made a careful examination of the small house, concentrating on the basement. Then he looked around in the barn. As he prowled around, flashlight in hand, he was constantly reminded of the prosecuting attorney's admonition that even if poison was found in the bodies of Lyda's former husbands, there would be no case unless a link could be established between the poison and the murderer. He redoubled his efforts to find something . . . anything that might point to the murderer of Lyda's husbands.

And Val Ormsby was becoming more and more convinced that the redhead's husbands had, indeed, met with foul play.

But if there was any hint of skullduggery to be found in the former abode of Lyda and her now-dead relations, it was not to be detected by Ormsby's prying flashlight. He thanked the young woman for her cooperation, then departed.

Little did he realize how much he had made Mrs. Lillian Johnson's day.

Chapter Four

Deputy Sheriff Val Ormsby made a tour of the nearby ranches, checking out the information he had learned from the young Mrs. Lillian Johnson. It was a time-consuming job that seemed to verify the reports from the new occupant of the Dooley house, but it all added up to very little additional information.

It was time to check out the farmhouse occupied by one Alfonso Dooley, whose sons, Edward and Robert, had both expired under such mysterious circumstances. As a result, Ormsby now found himself several states away in a bleak, desolate farmhouse in a farming community known as Keytesville, Missouri. Ormsby was hardly prepared for the grim-visaged incarnation of vengeance that faced him in the kitchen of the house.

"High time you people out there in Idaho did something about my boys," exclaimed Alfonso Dooley, his veins becoming cords in his neck. "High time. I tell you, my boys were murdered! Sure as I'm sittin' here."

Ormsby held up a soothing hand. "We're just as anxious to get to the bottom of this as you are, Mr. Dooley. That's why I'm here." He pulled out a handkerchief and mopped his brow, looking at the old stove in the corner of the kitchen that seemed to be almost glowing red. "But I'm interested in knowing just why you think your sons were murdered."

The old man looked at Ormsby for a moment, raking the deputy's face with his eyes. It was obvious that his sons had meant a great deal to the old rancher, who now looked so small and forlorn in the big kitchen. His gnarled hands trembled as he spoke. "When Lyda and Robert brought Edward's body back home for burial, we had no reason to be suspicious. Lyda told us Ed had died after eating sardines and milk. We all know that's guaranteed to make a polecat puke. People die every once in a while from ptomaine poison. Seems a lot of people just don't know how to can food very good these days. So we didn't think nothing of it.

"But it was Robert's death so soon after that got me to thinking. I'm a widower, you know, and it sure started getting lonely around here. But most of all I guess it was the calm way that Lyda took the whole thing. She sort of pretended to be sorry, but when I looked into her eyes all I could see was hard steel. You know what I mean?"

"I think so," said Ormsby, mopping his face.

"There didn't seem to be no compassion. No sorrow. Not the way a young widow should act when her husband has just passed away in the shank of life."

"I understand what you're saying." Ormsby watched with dread as the rancher went over to the stove and threw in a couple more sticks of wood.

The old man returned to his rocking chair and sat down. "When Lyda brought Robert's body back, we couldn't help but be a little suspicious. My daughter, Mary, said something in Lyda's presence about how maybe Robert had somehow gotten some poison in his system. I remember I was looking at Lyda's face at the time, and all of a sudden all the color seemed to drain right out of it. I found myself staring into the most frightening eyes I ever saw in my life. Cold . . . and evil. Then Lyda got madder'n a wet hen."

"I didn't know," said Ormsby, sliding his chair away from the stove, "that Lyda had a temper."

"Temper!" Old Dooley's eyes swept to the ceiling. "My God, I guess she had a temper! She came to me after Mary had said what she said, and told me, 'Father Dooley, when I get back to Idaho I'm going to have Mary arrested. I'm going to make her prove what she said about Robert being poisoned.'

"I looked at Lyda in astonishment. Then I told her to go ahead and get a summons for my daughter. Have her arrested. But by God, she'd regret it. I'm a poor man, but I'd spend every cent I own to find out if there was anything fishy about the death of my boys. Lyda looked at me, saw that I meant business, and all of a sudden she did a complete switcheroo. She became real sweet, said we had all been through a lot, and our tempers were getting the best of us. She allowed as how we should let bygones be bygones, everyone be friends."

"Did you?"

Dooley rocked for a moment before answering. "No. After she had gone back to Idaho, her face kept hauntin' me. I couldn't sleep for thinking about that woman with the steely eyes. My two sons were under the sod, and I was convinced by the way Lyda looked at me that she had had something to do with it." The old man turned watery eyes on the deputy. "I wanted to open the case. Hire a good lawyer." He shrugged. "But I'm a poor man. Barely make a living from this poor Missouri soil."

"I understand," said Ormsby, feeling compassion for the withered, sad old man in the rocking chair.

"I looked into it. I would have had to hire an investigator, go back to Idaho, pay for analyzing the bodies of my two sons. I just didn't have the money. Besides," he looked down at the hands that were trying to make a nest in his lap. "I have a feeling my boys didn't find much peace with that red-haired vixen around. Maybe they finally found peace in the grave." He looked up at Ormsby, who had risen and picked up his hat. "Wouldn't do to disturb them now, would it, young fella?"

"No." Ormsby patted the old man on the shoulder, then headed for the door. "It wouldn't do to disturb them unless we have to."

The trip to Missouri had unearthed nothing in the way of physical evidence. But Ormsby's talk with old man Dooley and other relatives and friends of the deceased had certainly shed some new light on Mrs. Lyda Trueblood-Dooley-McHaffie-Meyer. Was it possible that this woman could be both a lovely young lady and the vicious shrew described by the Dooley family? Was she some sort of a female Dr. Jekyll and Mrs. Hyde?

Ormsby had pretty well investigated the life of Lyda Trueblood-Dooley. Now it was time to check out the McHaffie marriage. To do this, Val Ormsby found himself in the struggling vicinage of Hardin, Montana. For it was here that Billy McHaffie, Lyda's second husband, had expired in the year 1918. The deputy had no way of knowing it, but this trip was to provide a major twist in the mysterious circumstances that were surrounding the deaths of Lyda's husbands.

Deputy Sheriff Ormsby had no trouble finding the Hardin doctor who had attended Billy McHaffie during his terminal illness. Dr. W. A. Russell was completely cooperative as the two men sat in the doctor's office and discussed the case.

"Of course I remember Billy McHaffie's death. It's the kind of case a doctor never forgets. You must bear in mind that the flu epidemic was killing people by the score in those days. In fact, the latest count shows that more than twenty million people died of influenza worldwide. We had at least half a million deaths in this country alone." He sighed. "Doesn't seem possible, does it?"

"No, sir," agreed Ormsby.

"But I digress. Due to the epidemic, I was working day and night. During this time, I received a call to drive out to the McHaffie ranch, a few miles out of town. I got into my car and rode out. In the bedroom of the old ranch house were twin beds. Billy was lying on one, Lyda was lying on the other. Lyda complained of them both being sick. I examined Lyda, but oddly enough, I couldn't find anything wrong with her. Then I examined Billy. He was in a bad way, with a very high temperature."

"Are you saying Lyda had no temperature? No symptoms?"

The doctor nodded. "None I could find. But it seemed obvious to me that Billy had the flu. I gave the prescribed treatment, left some medicine, and requested that he be kept warm and well covered, and be given hot packs. Since Lyda seemed to be in good shape, I just told her to get lots of rest." He gave the deputy a half-grin. "Sometimes women get a little psychosomatic when tending to the illnesses of a loved one."

Ormsby grinned back at the doctor, as if he knew what the word meant. "Please go on, Doctor."

The doctor narrowed his eyes, bringing his memory into focus. "Let's see. It was on my second visit a couple of days later. Yes. I found Billy lying on the bed, completely uncovered. Lyda was still in the other bed. She seemed well enough to me, but still insisted that she was sick. She said she had just given her husband some buttermilk, a hamburger, and a hot toddy. It was obvious to me that Billy McHaffie was dying. He still had all the symptoms of the flu, and that's how I diagnosed the case. The next day he died."

A short silence was broken by Ormsby as he reached for a cigarette. "Is there any possibility . . . whatsoever . . . that McHaffie could have been suffering from some kind of poison?"

"Poison?" The doctor shook his head. "It never crossed my mind."

"In all confidence, sir, we are exploring the possibility that Lyda's husbands might have been poisoned."

"Poisoned! The devil you say! By whom?"

"That we're not sure of. As I say, we're only exploring the possibility. We are ruling out no suspects, however. Did you see anything at all suspicious regarding Lyda's conduct at the time?"

The doctor mulled this. "Other than my not finding anything wrong with her . . . nothing. Although, come to think of it, Lyda might have been accused of neglect. She wasn't taking very good care of her husband. She didn't seem to be too concerned as to whether he lived or died."

"I see." Ormsby lit his cigarette and blew a cloud of smoke at the ceiling. "Tell me, Doctor. Is it possible that some types of poison might create the same symptoms as those of the flu bug?"

Again the doctor dredged his memory. "It's quite possible that some poisons could emulate symptoms of influenza — cramps, vomiting, thirst, even convulsions and coma. Also, you must remember that scores of people were dying of the flu right here in this county. With the flu epidemic in progress, I naturally assumed it to be just another case."

Ormsby squinted at the doctor through the smoke curling from his cigarette. "Dr. Russell, do you remember talking to McHaffie at all? Do you remember him saying anything?"

The doctor shook his head. "It's been some time ago. As best I can remember, he said little or nothing. The man was just too sick." Then the doctor leaned forward. "Wait a minute. There was something. On my last visit I saw him staring at his wife. I may have imagined it, but I could swear I saw a very malevolent look in his eyes. Almost a look of cold hatred!"

"That so?"

"Come to think of it, I made a lot of house calls in those days. Not many of them stand out. But the reason I remember the visits to the McHaffies is because there seemed to be such an atmosphere of tension. I felt that there was something cold and chilling pervading that sickroom. Something I couldn't quite put my finger on. Something tragic and mysterious." He locked eyes with the deputy. "That's no way for a coldly clinical man of medicine to be talking, Deputy. But, by God, that's the reason I remember the McHaffie visits so well."

Ormsby butted his cigarette. He thanked the doctor profusely for his cooperation, then rose.

"There's something else that might prove of interest," said the doctor, seeing Ormsby to the door. "Rumor has it that Lyda tried to collect Billy's insurance money after his death, but that the insurance had lapsed without her knowledge. So poor Lyda didn't get a thing."

Ormsby gripped the doctor's hand, and as he went out the door he threw back, "Poor Lyda. My heart goes out to her."

"Yes," said the doctor, closing the door. "Poor Lyda."

It took some digging to find the local insurance agency that had handled Billy McHaffie's insurance, but Ormsby's diligence finally paid off. The insurance agent was an unctuous man with a weak handshake and strong breath.

He looked up his records and confirmed that the doctor's report concerning McHaffie's life insurance policy was correct. The insurance had been allowed to lapse, but after Billy's death Lyda had hurriedly sent the back payment to the insurance company. She had then put in her claim for the five thousand dollars due on his policy.

"Ain't that the limit?" said the insurance agent, looking up from the file. "That young Mrs. McHaffie had sent in her overdue payment the same day I read in the paper of Billy McHaffie's death." He grinned. "I just had to tell that young lady that it was not our habit to renew life insurance policies on dead people. You know what?"

"What?" asked Ormsby.

"Must have hurt her feelings. Because I never saw her again."

"I'll take the call, Operator." Nellie Ormsby took off her apron and flung it over a kitchen chair.

"Hello, Nellie," said the voice that sounded as though it were issuing from a deep well.

"Did you say this was a Virgil Ormsby calling? The name sounds familiar. I'm trying to connect it with a face."

"Come on, Nellie. Quit clowning. I'm calling from the noisy lobby of this hotel, and our connection is terrible."

"Virgil Ormsby. I know now. I have a husband named Virgil Ormsby. I think. I haven't seen him for so long I wouldn't know for sure. Could you be he?"

"I'm just checking in, honey. Everything all right at home?"

"Just dandy. Where are you now? Missouri? Montana? Fairbanks, Alaska?"

"Now cut it out. I'm in Hardin, Montana. I'm just finishing up. I'll be home soon."

"Good. I'll tell the dog. If I can convince him you're not a stranger, maybe he won't bite you."

"Nellie, please don't act like this. I know I've been away a lot. But bear with me. I'm making progress on this case."

There was a pause on the phone. "Okay, Virgil. I don't mean to be a witch. But you've been gone so much, I might as well be married to a traveling salesman."

"I'll be home soon. I promise. We'll take a little trip together. Maybe go up to Lava Hot Springs."

"Promise?"

"Promise."

"Okay, Virgil. Be careful. And take care of yourself."

"You, too, honey."

Ormsby hung up, then climbed the stairs to his room. He hated hotels. Especially hotel beds. He took off his boots, pulled out a cigarette, lit it, and flopped down on the squeaky springs. As he stared at the naked light bulb glaring down at him from the ceiling, his mind, as always lately, went back to the case.

What strange new developments would await him on the morrow, when he paid a visit to the McHaffie ranch? Would he be able to come up with something that would justify his continued investigation of the case? He'd better unearth something concrete soon; his superiors were getting restless. He was running up one hell of a travel expense, not to mention the telephone bill.

And there was his wife. Nellie was definitely not a loner, and these absences from home sure weren't doing his marriage any good. He sighed.

His mind went back to the interview he had had that afternoon with Dr. Russell. He mentally compared it with the past interviews with the Twin Falls doctors who had attended Ed Meyer and Edward and Robert Dooley. In spite of the different diagnoses, the symptoms of the dying men had been quite similar. The only noticeable difference being in the case of McHaffie, who had suffered a high temperature.

As part of his homework, Ormsby had boned up on various poisons and their symptoms, thanks to the generous use of Dr. Coughlin's library. If this case did turn out to be one of wholesale murder, he might be able to identify the particular poison used. Then he would know what to look for. Arsenic was still high on his list, since it was used most often around farmhouses for rodent and pest control. But so far, he had found no evidence of poison being purchased by anyone who could be even remotely suspicious.

Yet, he kept recalling what the doctors had said about their patients prior to death. About the cramps in the stomach, the vomiting, the insatiable thirst. Even so, Ormsby had to admit to himself that these symptoms in themselves were not convincing. Although they occurred in arsenic poisoning, they were also symptoms present in innumerable diseases.

What the hell was he doing? Was he really on to something? Was he going to kick over an anthill of murder, mystery, and intrigue? Or was he on a wild goose chase, trying to track down someone who was perfectly innocent, and who would end up making him the laughing stock of Twin Falls, Idaho?

Sleep was a long time coming that night to Deputy Sheriff Virgil H. Ormsby.

The next morning Ormsby woke early, breakfasted at the hotel, and rented a motorcar. Snow had fallen during the night, and it was a slow and torturous drive through the drifts to the McHaffie ranch. At times Ormsby had to stop and shovel away piled-up drifts. It was early afternoon when he finally arrived at the house where Billy McHaffie had died.

He was met at the door by the Hannifins, a middle-aged couple who had bought the ranch from Lyda. He was ushered into the kitchen where a coal fire was burning. Ormsby wrinkled his nose as the smell of fresh-baked bread wafted through the house. Ormsby had worked up an appetite digging through the snow, and an offer of some hot bread and honey was eagerly accepted.

The couple was very friendly, hospitable, and willing to talk. The man, a tall rancher with a thatch of black hair, spoke slowly as he puffed on a briar pipe. "We knew Lyda and Billy McHaffie very well," he said. "They came up here and homesteaded this place about a month before we came out here. The crops were good that first year, and Lyda and her husband seemed to get along quite well."

"They seemed like very nice folks," said Mrs. Hannifin, watching approvingly as Ormsby wolfed down the fresh bread. "They seemed quite devoted to one another."

"And then something happened," said the rancher, stoking his pipe. "I think it's all right to talk about it, now that Billy's dead." He looked at his wife. "Don't you, Aimee?"

Mrs. Hannifin looked at her husband and nodded. "I don't see what it can hurt, dear."

"Well," said the rancher, obviously enjoying the conversation, "one day this man showed up. He was selling farm machinery. A real good-looker named Harlan Lewis. Jovial fellow, always laughing and cracking jokes. And there was something about him that really attracted the women."

"I'll say," said the housewife, pulling several more loaves of bread out of the oven. "He was real cute."

Hannifin ignored his wife. "He may have been attractive to the women, but there was something about that man that I didn't cotton to. Neither did Billy McHaffie. Anyway, Harlan Lewis gave Lyda one look, and she became a changed woman. It was almost like she had been hypnotized by this Swinegolly person."

"You mean Svengali?" asked Ormsby, using a piece of bread to clean up the honey on his plate.

"Could be. Anyways, Lyda acted like she was in a trance. She seemed to forget Billy entirely. She would look at Harlan Lewis like he was the only man on this planet. It was downright sickening. So I figured that if I had noticed the change in Lyda, Billy certainly had too. And from that time on, Billy and Lyda fought like cats and dogs.

"And hovering in the background was this fella Lewis. Always hanging around on one pretext or another. Aimee and I both got the impression that Lyda and this Harlan Lewis might have known each other before. It just seemed to me that he might have left her before Lyda married Billy, then came back to her. At any rate, she seemed absolutely under Lewis's spell. Like he was some kind of Swingolly."

"Svengali," corrected Ormsby.

"Anyway," said Aimee, refilling Ormsby's coffee cup, "when Billy McHaffie passed on, we got the impression that Lyda was mighty glad of it. And after his death, she sold us this place and just took off." Aimee Hannifin put the coffee pot back on the stove and smiled at Ormsby. "I suspect she went off with that Harlan Lewis. And I can't say as I blame her none. He had the most soulful eyes."

Hannifin shot his wife a look of disdain and knocked the ashes out of his pipe. "Whatever happened, haven't seen hide nor hair of either one since. They just up and disappeared." The rancher refilled his briar as Ormsby idly watched, his mind racing. My God! Here was an entirely new element in the mystery. A man he'd never heard of before — a ghostly apparition — had suddenly loomed up as a sinister and dominating figure who actually seemed to direct Lyda's actions! Some kind of Swingolly, as Hannifin had called him. Now where would this new angle lead? Was the busy little redhead now to be known as Lyda Trueblood-Dooley-McHaffie-Meyer-*Lewis*?

Or . . . Ormsby shook his head. His brain whirled back to earlier in the case when the possibility arose that someone besides Lyda might have been responsible for the deaths. When there might have been another party hovering in the wings, directing activities that had caused these mysterious happenings. Could this Lewis be that person who had been calling the shots? Lewis's presence in Lyda's life might explain why she had tried to keep her marriage to Ed Meyer a secret, fearing tragic consequences. Or . . . with an effort, Ormsby snapped these wild imaginings off before they drove him crazy. He cleared his throat and asked a question that was becoming all too familiar.

"Have either of you discovered any evidence of poison, of any description, since moving into this house?"

The rancher shot his wife a look, as her hands suddenly flew to her face, slapping her cheeks. As her eyes widened, Hannifin put down his pipe and said, "Aimee, I think we'd better show him."

Hannifin rose. "Come with me. Down the cellar. I have something that might be of interest. I don't know what it means, but maybe you can explain it."

Ormsby rose, his hands suddenly turning clammy. He watched as Hannifin took down a lantern, lifted the glass, and lit the wick. He tried to act calm as his heart hammered against his chest.

The rancher opened the cellar door, stooped over, and led the way down the winding stairs into the cold, damp vault, Ormsby hot on his heels. He then held the lantern aloft and pointed a long forefinger across the room. "See that barrel over there in the corner?"

Ormsby squinted to see through the dim light as eerie shadows danced on the mossy walls. "I see the barrel."

"That barrel was about the only thing left here by Lyda McHaffie when she moved. She may have just plum forgot it. Here. Take the lantern. Go over and take a look in the barrel."

Ormsby took the lantern, picked his way across the damp floor toward the old keg. Upon reaching it, he put one hand on the barrel's side, dipped the lantern into the dark void. His eyes grappling with the barrel's contents, he reached down and picked up an object. He stared at it for a moment, then, recognition flooding his face, he turned wide eyes on the face of the rancher.

"Well!" The words almost hissed as he expelled them. "I'll be a son of a bitch!"

Chapter Five

In the cellar of the bleak Montana ranch house, Deputy Sheriff Virgil Ormsby reached into the barrel and picked up one of the bundles that was illuminated by the flickering lantern. The paper was cut in squares, coated by some kind of sticky liquid. He let out a long, low whistle and punctuated it with one word. "Flypaper!"

"Yep," said the tall rancher, obviously relishing the revelation. "Bundles and bundles of flypaper. What does it all mean? We have flies around here, of course, but not enough to justify that much flypaper."

Ormsby ignored the question, raised the lantern, and started looking around the dank cellar. "Do you know if Lyda left any pots or pans here when she left?"

The rancher's look turned to one of puzzlement. "She left cooking utensils upstairs. Dishes, pots and pans. We've been using them since she left."

"How about an old bucket? Or maybe a stray pot she could have used for boiling?"

"Not that I know of. But there's a pile of refuse over there in the corner that they left. Been meaning to get down here and clean things — "

"Thank God you didn't!" Ormsby headed for the pile of debris. He began pawing through the mound of old clothes, magazines, bottles, searching with one hand, holding the lantern high with the other. And then suddenly he stopped, wide-eyed. He pulled out a large aluminum saucepan. "Aha! What have we here?"

Dumbfounded, the rancher watched as the deputy inspected the pan in the lantern light, running his hands around on the inside. Then

Ormsby's eyes grew even wider as his fingers explored a corroded line near the top of the pan. "This may be it. By God, this just may be it!"

"May be what?" demanded Hannifin, his eyes bugging.

"This just might be what I've been looking for." Ormsby picked up the old pot by the handle and clutched it to his chest like it might have been the holy grail.

"Are you daft, Deputy?" sputtered the rancher. "Just what the hell are you talking about?"

There was almost a maniacal look in Ormsby's eyes as he planted them on the rancher. "It just may mean, if my theory is correct, that murder was committed right here in your house."

The rancher could only stare, his jaw swinging on its hinge. Then he said softly, "Shit oh dear!"

"Flypaper!"

"Yes, sir, Sheriff. Flypaper."

"You got me out of bed to tell me you found a bunch of flypaper?"

"That's right, Sheriff. I found a stack almost a foot high."

"So that's how you're going to catch our killer. You're going to use flypaper."

"Oddly enough, that just might be the way we catch our killer. Yes, sir."

Ormsby could almost hear the fuse sputtering on the other end of the telephone. "I think you'd better start explaining, Ormsby. From the beginning."

Patiently, Ormsby described the events leading up to his discovery. About his visit to the old McHaffie ranch house. The revelation of the flypaper in the old barrel in the basement. Then his finding the pot in the refuse pile in the corner of the damp cellar.

Sheriff Sherman hung on every word, and when Ormsby finally stopped for breath, he broke in. "Let me be sure I've got this straight. It's your contention that Lyda boiled the arsenic out of the flypaper and used it to dispatch her husbands?"

"Yes, sir!" Try as he might to project the cool facade of the police investigator, Ormsby could not keep the excitement out of his voice. "According to my sources, there's enough arsenic in that flypaper to do away with the whole state of Montana. Don't you see, Sheriff, we finally have our poison. And not only that, but strong evidence that links the poison with Miss Lyda."

There was silence on the other end of the phone, then, "So you think Lyda boiled the arsenic out of the flypaper, then planted it in the oatmeal of her husbands."

"Something like that, sir. After making sure they were properly insured."

"You know what you're saying, Ormsby? You're really opening up a can of worms."

"I know, Sheriff."

There was another long pause. "I trust you've requisitioned the evidence. The flypaper . . . and the pot."

"Yes, sir. I have them here in my room."

"Good. What's your next move?"

"I've got some unfinished business here. Want to check out some of the stores in the area, hopefully get a lead on who bought all of that flypaper. And I want to get more background on this Harlan Lewis fellow, that Lyda was supposed to be ga-ga over. Looks like I'll be here a couple more days."

"Okay, Val. This new discovery should warrant some more time on the case. I'll notify the prosecuting attorney."

"Thanks, Sheriff. And would you do me one small favor?"

"Probably not. Name it."

"Call my wife. Tell her it doesn't look like I'll be home for her birthday."

"Oh, oh. That's bad news."

"You don't know how bad."

"I'll call her."

"Thanks, Sheriff."

"Just one more thing."

"Yes, boss?"

"Nice work, Val."

Returning to his hotel room, Deputy Ormsby pulled a small flask out of his old Gladstone suitcase and poured two fingers of bootleg booze into a glass. He took a long pull and wiped watering eyes. The goddamn busybodies who had passed the Eighteenth Amendment should be hanged, drawn, and quartered. Thanks to them, instead of relaxing in a nice saloon with good whiskey and a piano player setting a congenial mood, he had to drink green booze and stare at the cold walls of a hotel room. What the hell was this country coming to?

But Ormsby was not in a mood to dwell on the miseries visited upon the world by that old battle-ax, Carrie Nation. Especially with the glow of the grain alcohol that was beginning to warm his gut and tingle his toes. His attention was commanded by the newspaper-wrapped parcel sitting on his bureau. Finally. At last he had some solid evidence that would help forge the chain of circumstances that had surrounded Lyda Trueblood-Dooley-Meyer-McHaffie.

Vivid recollections flashed through his mind: the plodding through Idaho snowdrifts to reach inaccessible ranch houses in the hopes of picking up bits of information; the frequent challenges of men and nature as he tried to unearth the truth; his visit to Missouri and the home of the Dooley boys who had died under a cloud of mystery; he recalled the gaunt figure of old Alfonso Dooley who so poignantly decried the fact that no one was doing anything about the murder of his two sons.

And now this. Ormsby ran his fingers over the package. This bundle was going to compensate him for his hard work, his diligence that had tested his relations with his superiors; indeed, was putting a severe strain on his very marriage. Ormsby drained his glass, sat down on his bed. But he was still a long way from a locked-up case.

He wasn't positive of the identity of the killer. Or killers. Was it Lyda? Or could it have been Harlan Lewis, the latest figure to enter the case, and Lyda's alleged paramour? Or could these murders have been a joint effort? And where was the enigmatic redhead and her latest lover?

For all he knew, the killers might be here in Hardin at the moment. Plotting God only knew what in their next string of ghastly crimes. The word would soon spread that the flypaper had been found, and its arsenic may well have caused the death of Lyda's husbands. If so, the refugees would double their efforts to cover their trail. Now, time was truly of the essence. Or, as his favorite detective, Sherlock Holmes, might have put it, the game was afoot.

But first things first: a good night's sleep. He undressed and pulled his nightshirt on over his head. Then he reached into his bag for the gift his wife had slipped into it just before he left. He pulled out his brand new copy of Agatha Christie's latest book, *The Mysterious Affair at Styles,* and opened to the first page.

In this case, Hercule Poirot proved to be no match for Morpheus, who quickly whisked the deputy sheriff away from the Belgian detective and into the sleep of the dead.

After breakfast the next morning, Deputy Sheriff Ormsby took his room key to the desk. As he did so, the room clerk approached. Dispensing with the usual amenities, Ormsby asked, "How long have you been living here in Hardin?"

"About four years," replied the clerk.

Ormsby noticed out of the corner of his eye that a large man had approached the desk. Wearing a wide-brimmed hat and a fur-collared overcoat, the big man lit a long cigar. Ormsby lowered his voice, speaking in confidential tones. "Did you ever hear of a Lyda McHaffie?"

"Lyda McHaffie." The clerk's eyes suddenly brightened. "Yes. I knew her slightly. She and her husband used to come into town occasionally. Her husband had a ranch a few miles out of town. He died recently."

"Have you seen her since her husband died?"

"No. Can't say as I have."

Ormsby had the uncomfortable feeling that the big man hovering near the desk was eavesdropping on their conversation. He tried a new tack. "Did you ever hear of a man named Harlan Lewis? Sells farm machinery."

The clerk shook his head. "No, sir. You see, I've only worked at the hotel here six months. Don't recall that name being registered since I've been here."

"No Harlan Lewis."

"No, sir. As I say, I've only been at the hotel here a short while. Before that I worked at the drugstore."

"Oh?" A slight gleam touched Ormsby's eyes. "The drugstore." He leaned toward the face of the clerk. "Did the McHaffies ever come into your drugstore?"

"Oh, yes. Every once in a while. They'd always order a sarsaparilla at the soda fountain."

"Do tell." He leaned even closer to the clerk's face. "Do you remember ever selling them any flypaper?"

"Flypaper?" The clerk's eyes clouded.

"Flypaper."

"No, sir. Can't remember if I did. It was quite a while ago, and all I remember was Mrs. McHaffie being a cute little woman with big blue eyes. Afraid I can't remember what they bought."

"I understand."

"May I ask why you want to know, Mr. Ormsby?"

Ormsby dismissed the question with a wave of his hand, at the same time trying to clear the air of the cloud of strong tobacco smoke that was issuing from the big man standing behind him. He thanked the clerk, left his key, and tried to get a good look at the man with the big cigar and the turned-up coat collar. Unsuccessful, he headed for the garage where his rented car was parked.

A short time later Deputy Sheriff Ormsby was in the office of Dr. Russell, the physician who had attended Lyda's third husband. No, the doctor had never heard of Harlan Lewis, nor could he throw any light on the stacks of flypaper found in the old McHaffie ranch house. Then Ormsby asked the doctor about arsenic poisoning. Wondering what would be the most diplomatic way to phrase it, he decided to come right out with it. "Doctor, are the symptoms of arsenic poisoning close enough to those of influenza that you could possibly have made a mistake in your diagnosis of Billy McHaffie's death?"

Knowing that his professional judgment was being questioned, Russell thought for a moment before answering. "In all honesty, I could have made a mistake. But please bear in mind the circumstances surrounding my diagnosis. First, poison is rarely considered in a diagnosis, unless one has reason to expect the presence of same. I had no reason, whatsoever, to suspect foul play in the case of Billy McHaffie."

"I am not for a moment questioning your professional competence, Doctor. I — "

The doctor stopped him with a pointed finger. "Let me continue, sir. Secondly, remember that we were in the grip of a terrible flu epidemic. I had signed God only knows how many death certificates due to the disease that was ravaging our country. To answer your question, it is quite possible that a mistake could have been made."

"I very much appreciate your candor, Doctor. Let me reassure you that I have no wish to impugn the fine reputation you have in this community."

The doctor breathed easier. "I appreciate that, sir."

"I would be grateful, however, if you can answer a couple of questions about arsenic as a poison."

"I'll be happy to help if I can."

"Were we to exhume the bodies of Lyda's husbands, would we able to ascertain the presence of arsenic in an autopsy?"

"Indeed, yes. You see, Deputy, arsenic is an inorganic irritant. It's soluble in boiling water, and it's almost odorless and tasteless. A murderer using arsenic as a poison would be able to dispatch his victim without creating suspicion. There is, however, one serious drawback to using arsenic as a poison."

"And that is?"

"A body could be buried for centuries, but if exhumed, it would still show evidences of arsenic. It would be found throughout the tissues, the digestive organs, the bones, the hair, the brain . . . even the fingernails."

Ormsby released his tight grip on the arms of his chair and started to rise. He was unsuccessful in aborting the grin that creased his face. "Thank you, Doctor." He reached for his hat and headed for the door. "I won't take any more of your time. Thank you very much."

Deputy Val Ormsby spent the remainder of the morning calling at Hardin stores where flypaper might have been sold. But he found no evidence that either Lyda or Harlan Lewis had ever purchased any.

Heeding the gnawings of his inner man, Ormsby went back to his hotel for lunch. As he downed a thick slab of apple pie, he noticed the big man in the wide-brimmed gray hat that had hovered over him at the hotel desk. The man took a seat at a nearby table, and Ormsby had the uneasy feeling that he was being closely watched.

Any uneasiness the deputy might have felt was quickly buried under the avalanche of information he had just received from Dr. Russell. He had a hunch. If he were going to dispatch someone with a stack of arsenic-loaded flypaper, would he buy it in his hometown? Hardly. He would have gone farther afield than Hardin to purchase the murder weapon.

And the closest large town to Hardin? Billings, Montana. Furthermore, Ormsby's morning inquiries among the Hardin citizens had unearthed the fact that Lewis, the machinery salesman, made his headquarters in Billings.

That afternoon Deputy Ormsby boarded the train for Billings, Montana. Ormsby liked to ride the train. Especially in the smoking car. There was something about the smell of tobacco mixing with the acrid smoke that belched from the steam locomotive that one could almost taste. He took a seat by the window, nudged a gleaming cuspidor out of the way to make room for his suitcase. As he lit up, he watched the snow-dusted landscape fly by. He hiked his feet up on top of his suitcase, which contained the bundle of incriminating evidence taken from the McHaffie ranch house, and took a deep drag from his cigarette.

The rocking motion of the train had almost lulled him to sleep when he was brought to attention by a cinder in his eye. Moistening a corner of his handkerchief with his tongue, he deftly removed the train's smokestack effluvium. Pocketing his handkerchief, he felt the presence of another person entering the smoking car. His vision restored, Ormsby looked over to see a big man sitting in the far corner of the smoker, his suitcase in his lap, upon which the man was dealing a hand of solitaire. From time to time, somber eyes appraised the deputy from under a gray, wide-brimmed hat.

Reaching Billings, Ormsby hurried to the main hotel, deposited his bundle in the office safe, and was just about to repair to his room when he collided with a man approaching the desk. Muttering an apology, Ormsby found himself looking up into the somber face of the man wearing a coat with a turned-up fur collar, and a gray, broad-brimmed hat. "Excuse me," said Ormsby.

"Don't mention it." The eyes bored into Ormsby's as the man brushed a cigar ash off his coat. "You're Mr. Ormsby. Right?"

Taken by surprise, Ormsby returned the man's glare. "I am."

"Would you mind telling me," asked the big man, drawing himself up, "just what the hell is your game?"

Ormsby looked up at the broad-shouldered stranger, who towered at least a head above him. "I beg your pardon?"

The stranger thawed his face with a slight grin. "I think we should talk." He pointed to a couple of chairs in the far corner of the lobby. "Will you join me over there where we can converse quietly?"

Orsmby nodded curiously, followed the big man over to the chairs. They both sat down. The stranger crossed his legs, leveled his eyes at the deputy. "Mr. Ormsby, I have a feeling in my gut that says you're a lawman. Am I right?"

"That is correct, sir. Deputy Sheriff Virgil Ormsby from Twin Falls, Idaho, at your service. With whom am I speaking?"

"That is not important. I figured you as a lawman when I overheard you asking the hotel clerk in Hardin about Lyda McHaffie. And then when you asked about Harlan Lewis, I was convinced."

"I've noticed you tailing me. May I ask why?"

"I'm not tailing you, Deputy. We just happened to be going to the same place."

"You sure about that?"

The stranger held up his right hand. "Positive, sir." He lowered his hand and fumbled around in his vest pocket for a match to relight his cigar. "But if you're interested in Harlan Lewis, I just might have some information for you."

The deputy looked at the man with renewed interest. "You know Harlan Lewis?"

"Indeed I do, sir. Harlan Lewis was a friend. He and I were in the same business — selling farm machinery. I always liked Harlan. But there was something fishy about his relationship with Lyda. Now I never told anybody about this, but since you are a lawman and obviously investigating these two, I feel it my civic duty to come forward with some information that might throw some light on your investigation."

Ormsby found himself on the edge of his chair, looking intently into the serious eyes of the big man. "If you have any information regarding these two, I would certainly appreciate hearing it."

"Well, sir." The man lit the kitchen match, held it to his cigar stub, and started puffing. "We'll start with Lewis. Do you know where he is?"

"No, sir. But I'd very much like to know."

"I can help you there. Harlan Lewis is six feet underground."

Orsmby stared, blinking at the informant. "You mean Lewis is dead?"

"I certainly hope so. They buried him right here in Billings. Furthermore, in my opinion, he was murdered."

In the act of lighting a cigarette, Ormsby held his burning match in midair. "My God!"

"I didn't like Lyda. From the day Harlan introduced us. She had a strange look in her eye. I first met her when they came back from their honeymoon."

"Then they were married?" Ormsby winced as the burning match singed his fingers. He shook it out, ignoring his cigarette.

"Yes. They were married in Denver. In March of nineteen nineteen. They settled down, rented a place here in Billings. That same summer — I think it was in early July — Harlan caught the flu. He lived only a few days."

"Oh, my God!"

"Before he died, Harlan had confided in me that he had taken out a ten-thousand-dollar life-insurance policy. It was payable to Lyda. For some reason that aroused my suspicion. But that was not all. I went to see Harlan when he was sick. And you won't believe what I saw." The man blew a cloud of smoke at the ceiling.

"For God's sake, continue, man!"

"Would you believe Lyda had her clothes all packed, ready to leave? She told me she was sure Harlan wasn't going to get well. Now is that any way for a doting wife to act?"

"Our busy redhead has never been accused of being a doting wife."

"She was right. Harlan didn't get well. As soon as he was buried, Lyda vanished into thin air. I haven't seen her since."

Speechless, Ormsby could only stare at the big man.

"I'm glad to get this off my chest. It's been nagging me for a long time. I'm almost positive Harlan was done in by his wife. But having no evidence, I just kept it to myself. Now that I've come forward, I hope this information will be of some help. At any rate, I certainly feel better."

Ormsby shook his head, trying to clear it. "You've certainly done the right thing, sir."

The big man rose. "You can check out the facts I've given you. You might like to start with Dr. Wernham here in Billings. He attended Lewis during his illness. You may want to go out to the house where Harlan and Lyda lived and see the neighbors." He took a slip of paper from his pocket and scribbled on it. "Here's the address. I'll also put down the name of the insurance company, and the company Lewis worked for. Okay?"

"Okay." His mind racing, Ormsby reached for the slip of paper. Mentally comparing dates, he figured Lyda had married the farm machinery salesman about six months after she had buried Billy McHaffie. My God, what a busy little beaver! His mind returned to the present. "Sir, for my investigation report, I'd very much like to have your name . . . ."

Ormsby found himself staring at an empty chair. Looking wildly around him, there was no evidence the big man with the turned-up fur collar and the gray, broad-brimmed hat had ever been there, save for a dark pall of cigar smoke that hung like haze over the empty chair.

Deputy Ormsby felt a touch of déjà vu as he was ushered into the office of Dr. Wernham. He had visited so many doctors' offices of late that he was beginning to feel like a terminal patient.

The gray-maned, elderly gentleman did recall treating Harlan Lewis for influenze about a year and a half before. "Lyda Lewis," the doctor recalled, a twinkle coming into his somber eyes. "Now there was a pretty little filly. You ever meet her, Deputy?"

"Yes, sir. Years ago."

"Cutest little thing you ever saw. The way that red hair shone in the sunlight . . ."

"You we're telling me about Harlan Lewis, Doctor."

"Oh, yes. Well, Lyda suggested that her husband had eaten something that had given him severe indigestion. In his weakened condition, he had fallen prey to the flu virus. By the time I saw him he was so far gone we just chalked up Lewis's death to influenza."

The short interview with the doctor had shed no new light on the case, other than the fact the good doctor had been smitten by the vivacious redhead. Ormsby thanked the medic for his time, and spent the rest of the day verifying the information the tall stranger had given him.

A check at the courthouse confirmed the marriage had taken place, and a visit to the insurance agent also verified that the sum of ten thousand dollars had been paid to Lyda Lewis. Further, neighbors around the old Lewis home stated that Lyda's prediction of her husband's demise had, indeed, been voiced by her. And immediately after the funeral Lyda had disappeared as though she had been plucked off the planet by a giant hand.

The setting sun was chinning on the horizon when Ormsby finally returned to the hotel. He had a leisurely dinner in the dining room, then went up to his quarters. He kicked off his boots, stretched out on the bed, and stared at the ceiling. He loved his job, but he was sure getting tired of hotel rooms. At least the light bulb in this prosperous Billings hotel boasted a lampshade.

He got up, undressed, slipped into his nightshirt, and pulled out the Agatha Christie novel. He found it impossible to concentrate on his fictional hero, faced as he was with a real, honest-to-God true baffling case of mystery and intrigue. He shut the book on Hercule Poirot, and before knuckling under to a deep sleep he gave a few thoughts to the morrow, when he was going to try and find the store that had sold Lyda Lewis the lethal flypaper.

Well into his rounds the next morning, it was the fifth store he visited that finally produced pay dirt. It came in the form of a tall, pockmarked man with a huge nose flanked by a pair of ears that would have been at home on an elephant. The man commanded the counter of a Billings drugstore. After Deputy Ormsby had identified himself and asked his question, the clerk grimaced as if dredging his memory were painful. "Yes. I knew Lyda Lewis. She used to do a lot of her shopping here. Pretty as a picture was she."

Ormsby felt his body stiffen. "Did she ever buy any flypaper, by any chance?"

"Flypaper?" Again the eyes looked pained. "Not that I know of . . . wait a minute. By golly, come to think of it, she did."

"Tell me about it."

"Well, it was some time ago. Back in the fall of nineteen eighteen, if I remember correct. The only reason I remember is that she bought so much of it. Come to think of it, she bought all we had in stock."

"Go on."

"It's coming back now. I remember asking her why she was buying so much when the summer was over, and all the flies were holing up for the winter. She just laughed and said that she hated flies more than anything in the world. And that she would put the flypaper in little bowls around the house. Knocked 'em deader'n a doornail."

Ormsby found himself mezmerized by the pained eyes of the clerk. "You sure that's what she said."

"Positive. Even after all these months, I'd swear those were her exact words." He grinned at the lawman. "You know, Deputy, there was something about that woman. When she talked to you, the words seemed to burn into your brain."

"So I understand."

"Well, according to the papers she's a widow now." The clerk leaned forward and adopted a confidential tone. "I don't mind telling you, Deputy, that little woman can park her slippers under my campcot anytime she's a mind to."

"I wouldn't," said Ormsby, giving the clerk a thank-you handshake, "be in any hurry to lure her into your bed."

His thoughts tumbling, Ormsby raced back to his hotel. As he packed his old Gladstone bag, he had trouble concentrating on anything but Lyda Trueblood-Dooley-McHaffie-Lewis-Meyer. She had to be one of the craftiest, most cold-blooded women of all time.

Her presentiment that Lewis was going to die, and her quick getaway after the funeral was a repeat performance of her affair with McHaffie and Bob Dooley. Ormsby came to the conclusion that this femme fatale had first poisoned Ed Dooley, back in the ranch house near Twin Falls.

When she had seen how easy it was to do away with a human being, she had quietly insured Bob Dooley and fed him a lethal dose.

The third death had been Lyda's own three-year-old daughter, after her marriage to McHaffie. Had Lyda really been so lacking in humanity that she had taken the life of her own child?

Now it had become almost too easy, as Ormsby figured it. It was a cinch to then knock off Billy McHaffie, then Harlan Lewis, then Ed Meyer. Had five men, and perhaps a little girl, actually been slain by this pretty, soft-eyed wisp of a woman?

As Ormsby pulled the straps tight around his suitcase and buckled them, he felt a pang almost of panic. If this were true, how many more had this gay coquette killed since she had fled Twin Falls? Perhaps at this very moment she was brewing the poison potion that would send another victim to the grave.

He now realized the urgency of the situation for the first time. The bodies of Lyda's known victims must be exhumed without further delay. Lyda must be implicated in these deaths, and a net spread out for her capture.

Ormsby boarded the train back to Twin Falls. As he took up his favorite spot in the smoker, he ruminated about the work that lay ahead for him.

He had to apprehend this deceptively appealing lady Bluebeard before she had a chance to strike again.

Chapter Six

Back home in Twin Falls, Deputy Sheriff Virgil Ormsby lost no time in calling a meeting of his superiors to apprise them of the events that had transpired in Montana.

As he finished his briefing, Ormsby looked across the room at his boss, Sheriff E. R. Sherman, and Prosecuting Attorney Frank Stephan. Finally the sheriff took a deep breath and broke the stunned silence. "Well, Val, I think you've kicked over the anthill."

"Indeed you have, Ormsby," agreed the prosecuting attorney. "You've given us what we need to proceed. We have enough evidence to exhume the bodies. We'll start with the remains of Ed Meyer."

"Very well," said the sheriff. "But I suggest we keep the lid on this. For two reasons. One, no use getting everyone all stirred up until we know for sure these men were poisoned. And secondly, I don't think we should tip off Lyda, in case she's somewhere in the vicinity. If she's guilty and gets wind of the exhumations she'll take off like a scalded duck. So let's keep this thing secret. I'll take care of the paperwork, and we'll dig up Ed Meyer at night. Agreed?"

The prosecuting attorney nodded. "Agreed. If it turns out that there's no evidence of poison in Ed Meyer's body, we'd look pretty stupid. If there are signs of poison, we'll make announcements to the press at the proper time. Go ahead, Sheriff. Lay it on."

The night of April 2, 1921, was a damp, dark night, the feeble rays of the moon blocked by low, scudding clouds. A big truck lumbered into the driveway of the Twin Falls cemetery and stopped. Three figures scurried out of the dark and headed for the truck as four men climbed out. The three figures were the cemetery sexton, Louis Snyder, and two of his hand-picked gravediggers. The men dismounting from the truck were Deputy Sheriff Ormsby, Coroner P. T. Grossman, Twin Falls chemist E. R. Dooley, and Idaho State Chemist Edward F. Rhodenbaugh.

Holding the smoking lantern high over his head, the sexton led the entourage through the tombstones. The men sloshed through the slushy snow in single file, the lantern throwing long, grotesque shadows to flicker and die among the headstones. Finally the sexton stopped, stooped down, and scrutinized a low headstone. "Here it is," he whispered, as if any loud noise might awaken the dead.

Unshouldering their shovels and picks, the gravediggers went to work. Scraping away the soft snow, they swung their pickaxes at the frozen earth. It was slow going through the frost line, and then shovels were brought into play as the unfrozen earth became more cooperative.

Ormsby watched the macabre scene silently, barely able to control his anxiety as the dirt flew out of the hole that was getting deeper and deeper. Nearly an hour later one of the gravediggers, up to his neck in the cavity, let out an exclamation as his shovel struck wood. In a matter of minutes, ropes were slipped around the coffin, and with a good deal of grunting, the men raised the casket to the surface. The moon peeked through the clouds to reveal an eerie cortege as the grave robbers filed back to the truck, carrying the damp, earth-bedecked final repository of the ill-fated Ed Meyer.

Once inside the truck, the coffin was secured, the four men climbed back into the vehicle, and it headed out of the cemetery. It was well past midnight, and nearly all the lights in Twin Falls had flickered out. The truck growled through the back streets of the city until coming to the rear entrance of Coroner Grossman's undertaking parlor. Then one of the men jumped out, guided the truck as it backed up with its cargo. The coffin was carried inside, shades were pulled down, and the lights turned on.

A quarter of an hour later the frozen body of Ed Meyer was resting on a mortuary slab. Lying on its back, its face toward the ceiling, the body showed little signs of decomposition. Ormsby's heart was banging in his chest as he looked at the long, angular form. The intensity of the moment slammed him as he confronted the dead man that he was convinced would verify a ghastly secret. Unlike the other men in the room, Ormsby had not seen too many dead men, especially old friends who had been buried for months. Hypnotized by the form in front of him, his eyes suddenly bugged, and he let out an oath. "Jesus Christ!"

"What is it?" asked Dooley, startled by Ormsby's exclamation.

"Old Ed! My God, he's perspiring!"

Dooley grunted, then grinned at the perplexed deputy. "Condensation. Bring a frozen object into a warm, steamy room and you get condensation. That's what is forming on the corpse's face."

Ormsby exhaled. "Thank God for that. I swear, Ed looks like he's about to say something."

"Not likely." Dooley spoke in almost reverent tones. "Val, I know how anxious you are to get the autopsy report, but this work can't be rushed. You do want our best work, don't you?"

"Of course," said the deputy, tearing his gaze away from the sweating corpse. "We'll have to have something that will stand up in court. I know it will take time."'

"You have our words on it. Dr. Rhodenbaugh, Coroner Grossman, and I will give this project our first priority." He looked over at the body that seemed to relax as it began to thaw. "The least we can do for old Ed, here, is to put him back where he belongs as soon as possible." The city coroner looked closely at the face of the deputy. It was rapidly developing an ashen hue. "I take it you haven't seen too many dead bodies, Deputy Ormsby."

Ormsby cleared his throat and straightened his shoulders as he looked over at the coroner. "I haven't had this job long, Coroner Dooley. But I've seen a few in my line of work."

"Good. Did you know that coroners used to be called crowners in the olden days?"

"No."

"During the twelfth century, aristocrats, not doctors, investigated deaths to raise revenue for the king. These coroners, as they became known, conducted inquests in which they tried to identify all unnatural deaths. If there was anything amiss, the deceased's property was seized for the crown. It took hundreds of years for investigations to move from the tax collector's office to the scientific laboratory."

"That's very interesting," said Ormsby.

"Not really. But the art of autopsy has come a long way since then. Give us a little time, and we'll come up with the information you want."

Orsmby nodded. "It's in your hands, gentlemen. But please notify me the minute you have made your analysis."

"You can count on it."

"I don't mean to sound overly dramatic, but time is very important. At this very moment we could have someone else being prepared to join our friend here. I'm afraid we have a very dangerous killer on the loose."

The men nodded silently. Then Rhodenbaugh peeled off his overcoat, leaned low over the body almost as if to sniff it. "I can tell you one thing," he said.

"What's that?" demanded Ormsby.

"This corpse. It is in a remarkable state of preservation. And you probably know that arsenic is an excellent preservative."

"So I understand." Ormsby bent closer, examining the dank face with its big nose, closed eyes, and drawn mouth. "Old Ed just might be about to tell us something."

The following days seemed like months as Ormsby sweated out the results of the autopsy. Although he knew this exacting work required a lot of time, he could not help but call the mortuary on a daily basis, bugging the researchers and seeking any bone of information he could gnaw on. The only response he could get was that the Utah state chemist, Mr. Herman Harms of Salt Lake City, had been called to join the team. And he had been informed that poison tests were being made on Ed Meyer's liver, spleen, intestines, and kidneys. And yes, he would be notified the minute the analysis was complete.

While he was awaiting the coroner's report, he was also sweating out the analysis of the black flypaper and the pot he had retrieved from the Montana ranch house.

But while chewing his fingernails, Ormsby was also quietly going about his business of trying to locate the missing Lyda. Trying not to stir up suspicion among the Idaho populace that a murderer might well be lurking among them, Ormsby continued his investigation.

The information he uncovered had to be carefully sifted, as so much of it was misleading. But all leads had to be checked out. One report had Lyda back in Montana. Another informant placed her in Coeur d'Alene, in the northern part of the state. A third report established her in Denver. Another person, claiming to be a friend of Lyda, said the redhead had told her just before leaving Twin Falls that she was heading for New York City.

Ormsby retraced his steps to the day she had left town after Ed Meyer's death, and checked the railroad station. He found out that Lyda had bought a ticket for Buhl, Idaho, a small town west of Twin Falls. He went to Buhl, checked with the ticket office there, and found she had bought another railroad ticket for Salt Lake City. There the trail hit a dead end.

It was on the third day after the exhumation of Meyer's body that Ormsby received a telephone call that snapped him to attention. It was a female voice calling from Boise, Idaho, speaking in low, well-modulated tones. "Sheriff Ormsby?"

"Deputy Sheriff Ormsby speaking," said Ormsby, doodling on a note pad.

"This is Mary Staples. You don't know me, but I'm a clerk at the Mode department store here in Boise."

"Yes, Miss Staples. What can I do for you?"

"You can do nothing for me. But perhaps I can do something for you. I have a friend in Twin Falls who told me you are looking for a woman named Lyda Meyer."

"Yes. Do you know her?"

"Lyda is an old friend of mine. I received a postcard from her just last month."

Ormsby broke the lead in his pencil. "Are you sure it was from Lyda Meyer?"

"Oh, yes. I know her handwriting. The postcard came from San Francisco."

"San Francisco!"

"Yes. She said she was having a good time."

"A good time?"

"Yes." There was an awkward silence on the phone. "Maybe I shouldn't be saying this Mr. Ormsby, but Lyda always was a little . . . shall we say . . . boy crazy."

"You don't say."

"I do. She especially loved men in uniform. Her postcard said that she was having a good time in San Francisco because there were so many cute sailors there."

"Sailors!" Ormsby allowed his adrenaline to settle before continuing. "What was the date on the postcard?"

"It was dated just about a month ago. I hope this may be of some help. Is Lyda in any kind of trouble?"

"You've been most helpful, Miss Staples. Would you do me a favor?"

"If I can."

"Would you be kind enough to put that postcard in a letter and send it to me here at the sheriff's office in Twin Falls?"

"I'll be happy to. If it will help find Lyda."

"I certainly hope it will. And thank you, Miss Staples. Thank you very much."

"Don't mention it, Deputy."

Ormsby hung up and leaned back in his chair. San Francisco! This might just be his hottest lead yet. If the postcard proved to be authentic, the city on the bay could well be his next destination.

As he chewed this, the phone rang again. It was the prosecuting attorney. Ormsby felt himself growing rigid in his chair as the familiar voice announced, "Val, I've just received the coroner's report. They have finished their autopsy on Ed Meyer." There was a pause, then, "I hope you're sitting down."

Ormsby snatched the first report out of the voluminous autopsy file that had just been delivered to his desk. His brow furrowed as he started wrestling with the medical jargon.

Twin Falls County
Twin Falls, Idaho

Gentlemen:

In response to the request of Hon. Frank L. Stephan, Prosecuting Attorney of Twin Falls County, I beg to submit the following report covering the results in the toxicological analyses for legal use of certain internal organs of EDWARD F. MEYER, deceased.

The specimens from which the analyses were made were secured in my presence, and sealed in glass jars. Said specimens were taken from the cadaver of Edward F. Meyer at the time of exhumation of said cadaver in the Twin Falls Cemetery on April 3, 1921. I brought the sealed jars of specimens to the State Chemical Laboratory at Boise for analyses, arriving there on April 3, 1921.

The following analyses, by mutual agreement, have been limited to a search for the drug known as arsenic and this report is concerned only with the results of such search for said drug arsenic.

Respectfully yours,
(Signed) Edward F. Rhodenbaugh
State Chemist of Idaho.

Ormsby flipped over the cover letter to expose the first page of the report:

ANALYSIS

SPECIMENS: Material was contained in two one-pint Drey Ever Seal Fruit Jars, properly sealed, and marked as follows:

No. 1. "Edward F. Meyer, specimen Liver and Kidney, 4/2/21."

No. 2. "Edward F. Meyer, specimen Large and Small Intestine, 4/2/21."

All the material was softened by decomposition and gave off a rotten, putrid odor. Owing to this condition no opinion could be formed as to lesions, congestion, etc. of the tissues. Careful examination with the eye revealed no foreign material such as crystals, powdery substances, etc.

From the jar containing portions of liver and kidney, small, approximately equal pieces of each were cut. These were mixed and chopped finely and 20 grams of this material was placed in a new Erlenmeyer Flask and treated with arsenic free Hydro-chloric acid and Potassium chlorate. This was then digested over a boiling water bath and the process carried out as described in Antenrieth and Warren's "The Detection of Poisons and Strong Drugs" page 117 et seq. After completion of the process of purification from organic matter the resulting slightly yellowish solution was subjected to the modified Gutzeit Test for arsenic, the most delicate and accurate test known.

By this method as little as .001 milligrams of arsenic can be detected. The Gutzeit apparatus was first set up and allowed to run with only the chemicals and test paper present. This was done to prove that no arsenic was present in any of the reagents. An aliquot part of the solution to be tested was then introduced and the mercuric bromide paper subjected to the escaping gases. The yellowish orange stain proved the presence of arsenic. This test was repeated upon other aliquot parts of the solution with the same results.

Another 20 gram chopped mixture of Kidney and Liver was digested in boiling sulphuric and Nitric acids (Method of Danger and Flandin) until a clear colorless solution was secured. Aliquot parts of this solution were tested by both modified Gutzeit and Marsh tests both being positive . . .

His eyes beginning to glaze over from trying to decipher the language of the toxicologist, Ormsby leafed through several more pages of analysis procedure and results to arrive at the final paragraph. He bolted up in his chair as he read:

CONCLUSION

From the results of the tests made upon the internal organs of the late Edward F. Meyer, I am convinced that the poison or drug known as arsenic is present in sufficient amount to establish the fact that a lethal dose of arsenic has been administered. The amount of arsenic found in the foregoing analysis, it should be remembered, is but a portion of the total amount originally ingested by the deceased since a part of it was undoubtedly eliminated from the body before death; some was distributed through unexamined muscles, tissues and organs in the body and some has since disappeared, owing to putrefaction of the tissues during over two years of burial. I cannot but conclude from the amounts I have found that there was originally more than enough arsenic present to cause death. As to its source, I cannot say, as it is found in sprays, Fowler's Solution, poison fly paper, etc.

The report was signed and notarized by Jeanne L. Anderson, notary public for the state of Idaho.

Ormsby waded through the rest of the file, then closed it, tilted back in his chair and propped his boots up on his desk. He was going to allow himself a few moments to savor the sweet smell of success.

So. The chemists had found enough arsenic in the various organs of poor Ed to have killed five men. Morever, a conclusion by one of the experts had indicated that the arsenic had been introduced into the body in a liquid form. The arsenic contents of the flypaper had been verified, and the saucepan had shown traces of the poison.

In other words, Ormsby's belief that Lyda had boiled the flypaper, skimmed off the liquid, and put it into food or drink served to her victims had been verified. There was now little question that he was stalking a murderer, the likes of whom had not been seen since the days of Jack the Ripper.

After allowing himself this brief moment of self-congratulation, Ormsby got busy. Interstate arrangements for exhuming the other bodies were initiated. As the bodies of Lyda's dead husbands were exhumed, and samples taken of their organs, permission was granted to dig up the body of Lyda's first and only child, Laura Marie Dooley.

The ground had thawed in the early afternoon sun when the cemetery caretaker began digging into Laura Marie's grave. He reached the small wooden box of a casket in a short time and, with his assistant, lifted it out of the grave. He pried it open while onlookers held handkerchiefs over their faces.

As Val Ormsby looked on, attending pathologist Hal Bieler reached in and lifted the musty, white-laced burial dress over the tiny head. The appearance of the corpse was startling. It was poorly preserved, the once soft flesh of a three-year-old toddler was withered and dried. The body seemed remarkably small. This fact was to later fuel speculation by the prosecution that the child, which neighbors claimed often was not fed well, had been starved to death.

Pathologist Bieler made a scalpel incision from the front of the neck to the lower abdomen. It was difficult to get enough of the kidney, stomach, and small intestines for the chemical analysis, but they tried to make do, Bieler dropping crusty slivers from the different organs into fruit jars, carefully marking each jar.

Once all the jars were sealed, Ormsby placed them in his car with the bottled organ specimens he had just received from the corpses of Lyda's third husband, Harlan Lewis, who was buried in Montana, and specimens from the corpses of the Dooley brothers, who had been buried beside Civil War heroes in a Missouri cemetery. Ormsby personally delivered his grisly cargo to the chemists and pathologists who were working on the case.

Although the laboratory tests found similar levels of arsenic in the hair and organ specimens that came from the adult male bodies, they found no trace of arsenic in specimens from little Laura Marie's corpse. Ironically, while the absence of arsenic in the tiny body showed that the child had not been poisoned, it also helped to prove that naturally occurring arsenic in the ground could not have leached into the corpses of the men — a theory Lyda's defense attorneys would eventually assert.

The incriminating evidence was properly presented and filed. On April 22, 1921, the sparkling-eyed, enigmatic Lyda Meyer was formally charged with murder.

Now all Ormsby had to do was find her.

Chapter Seven

Deputy Sheriff Ormsby stood on the forward deck of a San Francisco-bound ferryboat as it pulled out of the Oakland dock. It was dusk, and the San Francisco skyline thrust a jagged silhouette into the wispy fog. The damp breeze felt good on the deputy's face.

As the ferry nosed through the chop, Ormsby's mind was a tumble. The elusive murderess was not his only problem. He was having serious problems at home. His wife was taking a very dim view of his spending so much time on the road. He had again been accused of being obsessed by this sloe-eyed fugitive, a charge that, deep in his heart, he was finding hard to dispute. He *was* obsessed by this woman who was now the object of a nationwide manhunt. Or womanhunt.

Upon learning that her husband was taking off again for an extended trip, Nellie had really put her foot down. Accompanied by an ultimatum. Ormsby was going to start spending less time on the road, or he was going to start spending the rest of his time as a bachelor. Their parting had upset Ormsby, as he truly did love his wife. It was even more important than ever that this fugitive from justice be quickly apprehended. Not only to prevent further deaths at the hands of the alleged Lady Bluebeard, but to prevent an untimely and unnecessary divorce. His.

Ormsby had never been in a city larger than Boise, Idaho, and he was overwhelmed by the bustling grandeur of the cosmopolitan city of San Francisco. With the help of a friendly taxi driver, he finally located a small hotel that he thought might not break the budget of the Twin Falls county sheriff's office, and checked in. It had been a long day, and he was hungry.

61

He went into the hotel dining room and ordered a large steak with mashed potatoes and gravy.

After topping his repast off with a piece of rhubarb pie and a cup of coffee, he was contentedly picking his teeth with his celluloid toothpick when the waiter brought his check. He nearly choked when he saw the bill. It was well over a dollar. He left a ten-cent tip, grumbling about the high cost of living in the big city.

Still smarting from the exorbitant price of his dinner, he took a brisk walk to see the fabled cable cars, then returned to his room to dive into his nightshirt.

While awaiting his breakfast the next morning, Ormsby sipped his coffee and studied the postcard he had received from the department store clerk in Boise. Upon receiving the card, he had called Mary Staples to press her for any additional information she might have. The only thing the clerk could add was that she and Lyda had a mutual friend living in San Francisco named Dellaine Risley, and Lyda just might be staying with her. No, she had no address for the Risley woman.

This is why Deputy Sheriff Virgil Ormsby now found himself eating his eggs and hashbrowns in the dining room of a small hotel on Market Street in the city by the bay.

Armed with only the name of Lyda's friend in San Francisco, Ormsby knew he would have to solicit help from the local authorities. He duly presented himself to the San Francisco police, and was pleased to find that the California lawmen were already familiar with the strange case of the Idaho poisoner, a result of the murder charge declaration that had gone out over the wires.

With the willing assistance of the police and the postal authorities, an address was quickly located for the uncommon name of Lyda's friend, Dellaine Risley. Grabbing a map of San Francisco, Ormsby's hopes were high as he rented a car and scouted out the tiny apartment on Clay Street that bore the address of Lyda's friend. Parking in front of the flat, Ormsby felt his adrenaline pumping. Was he finally about to come face-to-face with the woman who was usurping such a large chunk of his life?

Ormsby's knock on the door was finally answered by a person dressed in hair curlers and wearing a filmy French negligee. "Are you Dellaine Risley?"

"My God, I should guess not." Ormsby could not have been more startled by the deep baritone voice that issued from rouged lips. "I'm the landlord here. Who in blazes are you?"

Taken aback, the deputy found himself stammering as he identified himself. "I have this address for a Dellaine Risley. She doesn't live here?"

"Doesn't, no. Did, yes. She's flown the coop, honey."

"She's moved out permanently?"

"That she has." Ormsby felt a wave of despondency wash over him. Not only had he missed his quarry, but he felt uncomfortable trying to deal with this . . . person. He had run across several people of confused sexual persuasion during his police duties, but he was not prepared for this man who wore a sexy peignoir that seemed to be molting and shedding feathers.

"When did she move?"

The rouged lips formed a bow as the landlord thought. "Sometime last month. Didn't even give any notice. When her rent was up, she was gone."

"Did she by any chance have a houseguest? A pretty redhead?"

Again the pursed lips. "She may have. Come to think of it, there was someone staying with her for a while. I didn't pay much attention, honey. Women don't really race my motor."

"Did Miss Risley leave a forwarding address?"

"No. She did say something about going to Los Angeles. That's all I know."

"Well. Thank you very much for your time."

"My pleasure, dearie. If you're going to be in town you might like to drop by the Pretty Pussy cabaret some evening. Just ask for Edwina. I'm in the chorus line of the floor show. I'll be happy to buy you a drink."

"Thanks, Edwina."

"Don't mention it, you handsome thing, you."

Grim-faced, Ormsby went back to his hotel, checked out, and took the night train south. The smoking compartment was full, so he found a seat on the observation platform. He lit up a cigarette as the limited raced through the coastal towns under a star-speckled sky.

As usual, his thoughts turned to his quarry as he reviewed the day's events. Had he picked up the trail a mere handful of days earlier, he might now have Lyda Meyer in custody. If. If. The littlest word in the dictionary with the biggest meaning. He could not surpress a deep, shuddering sigh.

Ormsby was beginning to feel almost a kinship with the woman he was pursuing. Maybe he was getting to know her almost as well as she knew herself. Was this seductive woman actually killing her husbands just for the insurance money? Not likely. The money involved was not all that much to be the sole motivating factor. There had to be another reason. Was she some kind of psychopath who actually enjoyed killing men? Was she capitalizing on the fact that men were drawn to her as inevitably as flies were drawn to the flypaper she used in committing murder?

These troubling thoughts commanded Ormsby's attention far into the night, until he finally knuckled under to the hypnotic influence of wheels clickety-clacking on the steel rails, and fell asleep in his chair.

A nightmare brought him climbing out of his deep sleep just as the train pulled into the Los Angeles station. He dreamed he was having a drink with Edwina at the Pretty Pussy cabaret.

Once again finding himself in a huge, strange city, Deputy Sheriff Ormsby located a modest hotel, checked in, and then reported to the Los Angeles police station.

Chief of Detectives H. H. Cline was very cordial to the lawman from Idaho, curious to get more details of the fascinating story that had come clacking over the teletype about the comely redheaded murderer. He also summoned Captain J. B. Fox of the fugitive detail and J. F. Nolan, a deputy-sheriff, to attend the meeting. Ormsby brought the men up to date, then added, "I stress the fact that this woman must be apprehended as quickly as possible. For all we know, she could be boiling a vat of flypaper as we speak. And I only have one clue, the name of the woman who was Lyda's friend in San Francisco, and who is alleged to have moved to your city."

Captain Fox's gray hair and horn-rimmed glasses looked out of place on a large, well-muscled body. "We'll do everything we can to help you, Ormsby," he said. "You and I and Nolan here will work together. We'll find this Miss Dellaine Risley if she is in this city. And hopefully she can lead us to your fugitive."

"I'm very grateful for your cooperation, gentlemen."

Leaving Chief Cline's office together, the three men made the Los Angeles post office their first stop. Everything depended on whether the post office had any record of Dellaine Risley. The three men waited with tense expectancy as a postal clerk combed through the records. After nearly ten minutes, the clerk returned, carrying a card.

"You seem to be in luck, officers," said the clerk. "We have the Los Angeles address of Dellaine Risley. Our records also show that your Miss Lyda Meyer has been receiving mail addressed to General Delivery, until just recently."

"Hot damn!" exclaimed Ormsby. He copied down the address, then clapped the clerk on the back. "What would we do without our great U.S. Mail Service? You're worth every penny of the three cents it costs to mail a letter these days. And don't let anyone tell you otherwise." The clerk shook his head and looked at the retreating men curiously as they exited his domain.

Dellaine Risley's address turned out to be a tiny apartment on La

Cienega, near Sunset Boulevard. Parking the squad car in front, the three men got out and entered the small courtyard surrounded by apartments. Locating the number given by the postal clerk, Captain Fox knocked on the door. His breath locked in his chest, Ormsby could hear footsteps behind the closed door. And then the door was flung open.

A brunette with hair clipped into a pageboy bob surveyed the three men with sparkling blue eyes. Small and slender, Miss Risley presented an attractive picture to the officers. Ormsby tried to swallow the frog in his throat as he asked, "Are you Miss Dellaine Risley?"

Question marks formed in the large blue eyes. "Yes, I am. And who are you?"

Captain Fox removed his hat and introduced himself and his fellow officers. Then, "We'd like to ask you a few questions, Miss Risley. May we come in?"

"No."

Fox was taken aback. "No?"

"No. The apartment's a mess."

"Miss Risley, we'd very much appreciate your cooperation. It will be much easier to answer questions here than down at the station."

She crossed her arms. "Ask any question you'd like . From right there."

"Very well. Do you know a Lyda Meyer?"

"Lyda? Of course I do. Why?"

"When was the last time you saw her?"

"Just a couple of weeks ago. Lyda stayed with me." Her brow furrowed. "Why?"

"Do you know where she is?" demanded Fox.

"No, I don't. Say, what is this all about? Is Lyda in some kind of trouble?"

"She may be in big trouble. We need your help, Miss Risley."

"Well, if Lyda's in trouble, I want to help."

"Good. Now tell us where Lyda Meyer went after she moved out of your apartment."

A troubled look flashed across the face of the pretty brunette. "I would like to be of help. But Lyda became interested in someone. Which is why she left."

Ormsby's heart sank. My God, another victim! "Who was this man?" he blurted.

The woman addressed Ormsby. "Lyda liked romantic men. And she had no trouble attracting them. Her latest conquest was tall, dark, and very handsome. I think he was a Spaniard. Or maybe a Mexican. He was a gambler, and dressed very elegantly."

"Did this Latin lover have a name?" asked Fox.

"You won't believe this, but he was called El Zorro."

Fox stared at the woman, not blinking. "El Zorro? You have to be kidding."

She shook her head. "I'm not. Lyda referred to her new boy friend as 'My Zorro.' She went off with him a couple of weeks ago, and I haven't seen or heard from her since."

Ormsby thanked the woman for her cooperation, and as the three officers walked toward their car, Fox suddenly took Ormsby's arm and stopped.

"Do you know," asked Fox, "that Mex has the same name I have? Zorro is Spanish for fox. That dude is giving me a bad name."

"We can't have that," said Ormsby absently, his mind on other things.

"We have quite a Mexican colony here in L.A. Nolan and I know it pretty well. We'll go down there and see what we can find out about this Zorro dude."

"Good," said Ormsby. "I'll go with you."

"No," said Fox. "Our informants don't like strangers. We'll have better luck if Nolan and I do this by ourselves. You go back to your hotel room and wait for our call. We'll stay in close touch."

Ormsby was on the verge of arguing, but he could see the wisdom of Fox's decision. He allowed himself to be deposited at his hotel.

It was late. Pacing back and forth, Ormsby had all but worn a path in the thin carpet of his hotel room. He was just about to get ready for bed when the phone rang. He leaped on it. "We're down in the lobby," said Fox's voice. "Be up in a minute. I think we're on to something."

"Come on up," said Ormsby, unable to keep the excitement out of his voice.

Moments later the two detectives strode into the room. Fox sailed his hat onto the bed and plunked down, weariness etched in his face. "Got anything to drink?"

Ormsby moved to his suitcase and produced his small flask. "I've got some green sour mash." He rinsed out two glasses in the sink, sloshed some booze in them, added a little tap water, and handed them to the lawmen.

Fox took a long draft, then screwed up his face. "That rotgut would gag a goat."

Ormsby nodded. "You may notice that I'm not drinking any. What did you find out?"

"Well," said Fox, bracing himself for another swig. "We got one of our stoolies to talk. It seems our boy Zorro is a high-stake gambler, and has a great eye for women. He's a Mex, not Spanish. He was seen with a woman fitting Lyda's description in several of the Mexican restaurants. Up to about two weeks ago. Then they both disappeared."

"Go on," said Ormsby, his voice quivering. Fox took another drink, wiping watering eyes. "Don't drink, talk."

Fox cleared his throat. "We checked several of the restaurants frequented by Mr. Zorro. At the last one, we got a break. We found a manager who said he was a friend of our mystery man. He said Zorro had gone south, taking the woman with him. They were heading for the border. He said they were going to stop at Tijuana, maybe head on south to Mexico City. They left in an expensive sedan, which the manager thought belonged to the woman."

"My God!" said Ormsby, digesting this information. Fox drained his glass and picked up his hat. As he stood up, Nolan lifted himself out of the only chair in the room and picked up his hat. "So tomorrow," said Fox, "we head south. Ever been to Tijuana?"

"No."

"Miserable damn border town. But they make tequila that beats the hell out of this rotgut. We'll leave in the morning. Early start. Pick you up here about six a.m. Okay?"

"You bet."

Fox headed for the door, followed by Nolan. As he went out the door he shot back, "Ormsby, about your booze. If you're smart, you'll fire your bootlegger."

Chapter Eight

It took over an hour for Deputy Sheriff Ormsby to get his call through, and when he finally did the phone rang a long time before his wife responded in a sleepy voice.

"Hello, sweetheart. Is this the love of my life?"

"Who is this?"

"It's your husband. How many men call you sweetheart?"

"You'd be surprised. Why are you calling at two in the morning?"

"I'm sorry, honey. I just got through with a meeting. I wanted you to know that I'm leaving early in the morning for Tijuana."

"Tee-what?"

"Tijuana. It's just across the Mexican border."

"*Mexico!* What the devil are you going to do in Mexico?"

"We have a lead on Lyda Meyer. We think she's in Mexico."

"Great God Almighty!"

"I'm truly sorry, honey. I know I promised to be home for our anniversary. But we're very close to apprehending this fugitive."

There was a long silence on the phone, then, "Virgil Ormsby, you'd damn sure better be! This redhead is ruining our life. If you don't hurry up and find her, you can also start looking for another wife."

"Honey —"

The line went dead as Nellie hung up.

Cursing, Ormsby replaced the receiver. He thought for a moment, then picked up his flask and poured himself a large shot of sour-mash goat-gagging whiskey.

Shortly after daybreak the next morning, the open touring car pulled up at the curb in front of the hotel. Climbing in, Ormsby exchanged pleasantries with Detective Fox and Deputy Sheriff Nolan, then the three men headed south.

Reaching San Diego a few hours later, Fox turned the car toward the local Mexican quarter. Their search for information finally paid off in a nondescript cantina that served cold enchiladas and warm bootleg beer. The owner had seen El Zorro, accompanied by a pretty woman. They had left for Tijuana.

Buoyed with the scent of the chase, the three men flashed their credentials at the border police and drove into Tijuana. Threading through the vendors, the California lawmen grudgingly allowed Ormsby to purchase a few souvenirs for his wife, then the three men scouted out the Tijuana police station.

Completely ignored by several scrawny chickens pecking away in the gutter, the men walked into the dingy office and introduced themselves to the chief of police. When apprised of their mission, the mustachioed Mexican stated he knew nothing of the whereabouts of El Zorro or his woman. He did, however, offer his cooperation in helping to find them.

"Thanks," said Captain Fox, shaking hands with the chief, "but we'll do this on our own."

"*Muy bien, señor.* But be careful. Tijuana is a nice city, but it has an element that, shall we say, can be a bit unsavory."

"We'll be careful." He smiled at the officer. "And thanks for your cooperation."

The night life of the border town was going full blast as the three men strolled down the litter-strewn sidewalk. Deflecting the advances of ladies of the evening, the lawmen passed the doors of the gambling dens that were wide open in deference to the warm breezes that swept the town. The sounds of clicking roulette wheels mixed with the touts of hucksters trying to lure the men into the girlie shows.

Ducking into a cantina that seemed remotely respectable, Captain Fox ordered a round of drinks for the three of them, then spoke in a low whisper. "I rejected the police chief's offer of assistance because I think we can do better on our own. Without alerting the Mexican grapevine. I know a Mex gambler here named Sanchez. He's one of the local big shots. If anyone knows the whereabouts of Zorro, Sanchez will. And he owes me. He'll talk."

Ormsby studied the face of the burly policeman in a new light. He was gaining respect for this cop, who seemed to have connections in at least two countries. Back in his hometown of Twin Falls, Ormsby didn't have a single informant or confidant. He made up his mind that he was going to develop some stoolies immediately upon his return.

Fox went on to describe Sanchez to his fellow officers, then he skoaled his beer. "Let's split up. Nolan, you take the saloons on the left side of the street, Ormsby and I will take the ones on the right side. Just ask for Sanchez. We'll meet back here in an hour. Okay?"

The men nodded in agreement. Nolan deployed to his assignment, Ormsby fell in with Fox as the men started canvassing the saloons on both sides of the street. Elbowing their way through the crowds of panhandlers, pimps, and prostitutes, Ormsby flashed a nervous glance at the large detective by his side. "The police chief was right. Calling this place unsavory is highly complimentary."

Fox grunted an acknowledgement, adding, "Keep a good grip on your wallet. Some of these pickpockets could steal your B.V.D.'s and you'd never know it."

Hitting one saloon after another, the two men's modus operandi was the same. They talked to the bartender, the manager, and the bouncer, asking if they had seen Sanchez. The answers were negative, as the two gringos were eyed with suspicion. In the fourth bar they approached, one of the bartenders said he had just served Sanchez, but he had left, heading for another bar. The Mexican shook his head when queried about the name of the bar Sanchez was heading for. "I don't remember, *señor*."

"Maybe this will help jog your memory," said Fox, pulling a ten-spot from his wallet.

"*Si, señor*," said the bartender, surreptitiously palming the bill. "I suddenly remember. Sanchez was going to the California Cantina." He pointed down the street. "About two blocks down, on the right-hand side." He leaned into Fox's face. "And don't tell no one I told you."

"Our secret," said Fox, reeling from the burrito breath of the bartender. The two men headed for the door.

The California Cantina was a dimly lit bistro, smelling of stale beer and urine. A topless dancer with pendulous breasts that kept eclipsing her navel gyrated on a tiny stage above the backbar. Elbowing through a small crowd, the two men made their way to the bar. Captain Fox approached an obese man with slicked-down hair and teeth that parted in the middle. The man's flapping serape looked out of place with the manicured fingers that gripped a beer glass.

"Ah," said Fox, looking at the reflection of the Mexican in the bar mirror. "My old friend Sanchez."

Sanchez turned his eyes from the dancer, who was doing obscene things with the curtain, and planted them on the reflection of the men behind him. He swung around on his barstool. "Captain Fox!" A grin wrapped itself around the crooked teeth. "*Como esta, amigo?*" Sanchez clapped Fox on the back. "Let me buy you a drink, *amigo* ... "

"No thanks, Sanchez. Another time."

"*Muy bien.* But I owe you, *amigo.* For getting me off the pimp charge in L.A."

"My pleasure. We needed a man we could trust in Tijuana more than we needed another pimp in our L.A. jail."

"You got a nice way of putting things, *señor*. What can I do for you?"

"I need some information." Fox outlined their mission, describing Lyda Meyer and Zorro. When he had finished, Sanchez took a long draft from his beer and fixed watery eyes on the detective.

"I know Zorro." Sanchez nodded his head. "He is an interesting man. More gringo than Mexican."

Ormsby took a deep breath as he watched the Mexican over Fox's shoulder. "Do you know anything about an American woman who might be with him?"

The Mexican shrugged his shoulders. "El Zorro always has a woman on his arm. I know nothing about no American woman."

"Where can we find El Zorro?"

Sanchez took another draft from his beer. "I have heard rumors that he is staying in a house not far from here. On Negrete Avenue. And about Fifth Street. It's a white house with a big garage behind it."

"Walking distance?" asked Fox.

"For you, *señor*, yes. For me, no."

Fox patted the Mexican's huge stomach and thanked him. As they headed for the door, Ormsby asked, "What about Nolan?"

"We'll pick him up later. I don't want to waste a minute getting to that house."

Ormsby fell in step with the long strides of the captain as they headed down the street.

Leaving the main avenue, the two men walked swiftly down the dark side streets, pausing occasionally to check the obscured street signs in the dim light. Finally, Fox grunted and pointed at a house in the middle of the block. "There's a white house with a double-car garage in back. This must be the place."

Ormsby took deep breaths, trying to satisfy a pounding heart. "Lights are on. Seems to be someone home."

"Remember what Sanchez said. Zorro may get nasty if we bother him when he's with a woman. Unholster your gun."

Ormsby needed no urging. He drew his weapon, keeping it at the ready as they approached the run-down clapboard house. There was a light downstairs, but the upstairs was dark. Approaching, Fox suddenly stopped, Ormsby hard on his heels. The detective put his forefinger to his lips. As Ormsby nodded, he happened to glance up. At one of the upstairs windows he thought he could see the outline of a face pressed against the glass. And then, as quickly, it disappeared.

Fox quietly turned the handle of the front door. It was unlocked. Opening it, the two men tiptoed into the front room. An oil lamp was burning on a table in the corner, but the parlor was empty. An open door led off the hall to another lighted room. Stopping to cock an ear, Fox held up his hand to the sheriff. The two men stopped and listened.

Blocking the door, Fox said in a loud voice, "Hello!"

An old Mexican appeared in the doorway. He was wearing bib overalls and a gray shirt. The old man's eyes bulged as he saw the two men before him with drawn guns. "*Dios mio!*" He stared in amazement at the two interlopers, then his questioning look turned to one of hostility.

Fox took a step forward. "We're not going to hurt you, old man."

"*Dios mio!*" The Mexican wiped his sweating face with the sleeve of his shirt.

"We're looking for El Zorro."

Staring up into Fox's face, the old man's eyes suddenly turned from hostility to cunning. "El Zorro?"

"*Si. Donde esta* El Zorro?"

The Mexican shook his head. "El Zorro *no aqui.*"

"We know he lives here," said Fox in a quiet voice. "We are friends. We just want to talk to him. Now where is he?"

Fox reached toward the old man's shoulder. Just as he did, the Mexican wheeled, and with incredible speed he darted through the room and lunged out the back door.

Hot on his heels, Fox ran after him throwing an order back to Ormsby. "I'll go after the old man. You search the house."

Caught flat-footed by this turn of events, Ormsby took a fresh grip on his revolver as the thump of running feet subsided in the distance. He stepped into the deserted room of the Mexican, checked the dingy kitchenette that took up most of the room. Several cockroaches were fighting over a cold dish of frijoles on the table. He was checking out the closet when he heard the noise.

From overhead came the sound of quick footsteps. Then the squeak of a bedroom door opening. The footsteps, almost on tiptoe, started down the stairs. His hand shaking, Ormsby looked at the closed door that led upstairs. Getting a grip on himself, he watched the doorknob as the steps came closer and closer. From the sound, he knew there were two people on the stairway.

The footsteps stopped, just behind the door. And then, ever so slowly, the doorknob started to turn. Reaching the door in two strides, his gun leveled at the doorknob, Ormsby snatched the door open.

"Jesus!" said a surprised voice coming from the dimly lit stairs.

"Don't try anything," said Ormsby, "I'm from the police. I've got you covered."

In the light of the naked light bulb shining above the stairs, Ormsby could make out the figure of a tall, neatly dressed Mexican. And then, behind him, he made out the figure of a woman.

"Don't do anything dumb, gringo," said the Mexican, raising his hands. "I got no firearms."

"Come out here into the light." Ormsby ordered, motioning with his revolver.

The tall Mexican obliged, casting furtive eyes around the room.

"You too, miss," said the sheriff, motioning to the figure that hung back in the semidarkness. Ormsby had trouble breathing as his adrenaline whipped into high gear. Was he actually going to see the quarry he had spent months trying to find? "Out here in the light where I can look at you."

Slowly, the trim figure of the woman came into the room, staring with wide eyes at the man with the gun. She followed the sheriff's motions as he directed her near the lamp where he could get a good look at her. Ormsby moved closer, squinting at the woman. There was a long pause, then Ormsby exhaled. "Son of a bitch!" he said.

The Tijuana police chief lit a brown cigarette, then blew a cloud of smoke at the ceiling. His eyes took turns lighting on the faces of Captain Fox and Deputy Ormsby as they flanked the tall Mexican in the middle.

"Sorry to disappoint you, gentlemen, but the man you have handcuffed here is not El Zorro."

"Are you sure about that, Chief?" asked Fox.

"Very sure." The chief punctuated his pronouncement with puffs of smoke.

God, thought Ormsby, his nose wrinkling. He could not come to grips with the Mexican cigarette. It could only have been made from fermented camel dung. "This man certainly fits the description of El Zorro," he said.

The chief's mustache made a little V as he smiled. "*Señors*, shake hands with Juan Garcia. Juan is one of my undercover agents."

The mouths of Fox and Ormsby flew open as they turned to the manacled man between them. "No shit!" said Fox, staring blankly at the Mexican.

"Garcia," said the chief, "has been staking out the house of old man Gomez, who is running a whorehouse in his upstairs." Again the chief grinned. "As you know, we have strict laws against prostitution here in Tijuana. It has to be carefully monitored. We don't want your American gangsters muscling in here.'"

"Then I take it," said Fox, "Garcia was investigating the house when we entered."

"Precisely."

"I was just about to arrest this woman," said Garcia, "when you two gringos busted in."

"You have an interesting way of collaring prostitutes here in Mexico. I could swear I heard bedsprings squeak as we tiptoed into the house."

"I'm sure Garcia," said the chief, "was only doing his duty. Right, Juan?"

The tall man grinned. "Right, Chief." The Mexican held out his hands. "Now if you'll be so kind as to take off the handcuffs."

Embarrassed, Fox unlocked the manacles. "Please accept our apologies, Garcia. We had no way of knowing."

"That's okay. I'm just sorry the woman in the house was not your Lyda Meyer."

"So are we."

"I did pick up some news that might be of interest. Your man, Zorro, was staying at the house of Gomez."

A spark rekindled in the eyes of Ormsby. "Go on, Garcia. Tell us all you know."

Rubbing his wrists, the Mexican looked at the men. "El Zorro went south about a week ago. But there was no American woman with him."

"Are you sure?" asked Fox.

"My source is quite reliable. It's the old man you about scared the shit out of when you broke into his house."

"We'll consider that reliable," said Ormsby.

"El Zorro told old man Gomez that he needed work. And that he had heard of an opening as a croupier in a gambling house."

"And where is this gambling house?" asked Ormsby, his acute disappointment beginning to wane.

"Ensenada. It's a little town south of here on the coast."

"I know where it is," said Fox.

"I am sorry," said the chief, "that your mission here was not successful."

"Thanks, Chief," said Fox. "And thanks for all your help."

"Don't mention it, *señor*."

The two men shook hands with the Mexicans, then headed for the door. "Just promise me one thing."

"What's that, Chief?" asked Fox.

"Promise me you'll try not to arrest any more of my men."

Hailing a taxi, Fox and Ormsby gave the driver instructions to take them to their hotel. As they settled back in the seat of the rickety vehicle, Ormsby fought with a seat spring that kept surfacing between his legs. He turned to Fox. "So it's been a wild goose chase."

"Not necessarily," said Fox. "El Zorro may have dropped Lyda somewhere along the way, but only he'll know where. And chances are they've been in touch. At any rate, it's the only lead we've got. We'd better follow it and catch up with El Zorro. Don't you think so?"

"You mean go to Ensenada?"

"I do. We've come too far to back out now."

"Then let's do it." As Ormsby mulled just how he was going to tell his wife, his thoughts were shattered by an expletive from Fox.

"Good Christ!"

"What is it?"

"Nolan. I forgot all about Nolan. He's been waiting for us at that bar for hours!"

Ormsby grinned. "Knowing Nolan, he probably hasn't minded all that much. There are worse places to wait than in a lively bar."

Not one to let the grass grow under his feet, Captain Fox picked up Nolan, who was suffering no pain as a result of closing a Tijuana tavern. Then they picked up their touring car at the hotel. Smothering Nolan's protestations at embarking for Ensenada in the middle of the night, the two men loaded Nolan into the back seat, checked out of the hotel, and headed out of town.

His coat collar turned up to ward off the ocean breeze, Ormsby watched Captain Fox pick his way along the crude and hazardous highway that skirted the ocean. The road from Tijuana to Ensenada was a treacherous course, at times little more than a trail in the dry, boulder-studded bottom of a canyon, then precariously rising to the top of cliffs to overlook the booming surf of the Pacific Ocean.

A spindly moon peeked occasionally through the high fog that swept in from the sea, illuminating the savage grandeur. The beauty of the Mexican coastline was lost on the men, however. Nolan was dead to the world in the back seat, and Ormsby was busy jabbing the heavy-lidded Fox to keep him from falling asleep at the wheel as they searched for the lights of the coastal village of Ensenada. The sun was just beginning to test the horizon when the touring car pulled into the sleeping village.

"Is that you, Sheriff Sherman?"

"It's me, Ormsby. Where the hell are you calling from? Sounds like you're in an outhouse."

"I'm calling from the police station in Ensenada, Mexico. We seem to have a very bad connection."

"You're still in Mexico?"

"Yes, sir. We're following a tip that El Zorro might have been in Ensenada. The police chief says he was here alright. We just missed him by several days."

"That's too bad."

"Yep. But we have a reliable report that Zorro is in Mexicali."

"Mexi-what?"

"Mexicali. It's a town on the Mexican border. We have a hot tip that Zorro is working in a casino there."

"Good God, Ormsby, you're doing more traveling than Phileas Fogg."

Ormsby had to think a moment before he placed the hero of Jules Verne's novel, *Around the World in Eighty Days*. He was, indeed, seeing the world on this mission. "Sorry, boss. But Zorro is the hottest lead we've got. I don't want to come back empty-handed. Besides, Mexicali is on the way home."

"Okay. But you're sure as hell putting a hole in our county travel budget."

"I realize that, sir. Would you do me one small favor?"

"Name it."

"Please call my wife. Tell her I'm on my way home."

"I'll do it."

"Thanks, Sheriff. *Adios*."

"*Adios?*"

Since he was the only one who had had any sleep, Nolan was pressed into service behind the steering wheel. The begrimed touring car headed for the Mexican border. The lawmen passed through Tijuana, gassed up, and headed for California's Imperial Valley. A blazing sunset painted its weird green and lavendar pastiche in the sky as the car bumped along the wooden highway toward Mexicali.

It was well after dark when the tired, disheveled men pulled into Mexicali and located the police chief's office. Looking more like felons than law officers, the men presented themselves to the chief. Captain Fox explained their mission.

The Mexicali police chief was a squat man with a pencil-line mustache on his upper lip. He wore riding breeches tucked into high riding boots bedecked with silver spurs. As he spoke, he emphasized his thoughts by slapping his leg with a riding crop carried in his right hand. He exuded the pungent aroma of horseflesh, obviously more at home with the four-legged oat chomper than the four-wheeled gas guzzler.

When Fox finished, the police chief settled back in his chair and surveyed his visitors. "So you're looking for the man, El Zorro."

"That's right," said Captain Fox. "We just want to talk to him."

"That can probably be arranged, gentlemen," said the chief, producing a cigarette and lighting it. Ormsby winced; he knew the God-awful smell of Mexican cigarettes would soon assail his nostrils. "Your El Zorro is here."

Ormsby's ennui was shattered as if he had just been hit with a bucket of ice water. "Are you certain?" he snapped.

"I'm certain. We keep an eye on all strangers that come to town. And everyone knows El Zorro."

"Does he have an American woman with him?"

The police chief stared at the deputy sheriff, whose nerves seemed tauter than a guitar string. "I know of no American woman. But I do know that El Zorro is running a roulette wheel over at the Owl Gambling House. I can have him picked up."

"Splendid," said Captain Fox. "Will you be kind enough to do that?"

The Mexican nodded, and excusing himself, went out the office door. As the jangling of the chief's spurs faded down the hall, the room turned deathly quiet. Only the sigh of a consumptive ceiling fan violated the silence. All but Ormsby were relaxed. Fox produced a cigar and lit it, blowing smoke rings at the lazy fan. Nolan sank heavily into a chair, massaged his temples, fighting sleep. Ormsby rose, pulled out a bandana, and wiped the sweat and grime from his face as he nervously paced the floor.

All sense of fatigue had been drowned in the adrenaline that rushed through Ormsby's veins. The noise coming through the open window of the crowds in the Mexicali streets barely registered as he thought of El Zorro and the possibility of a lead that might, at long last, take him to Lyda Meyer.

The Mexicali chief came back into the office, trailing a veil of cigarette smoke. Ormsby coughed into his bandana as the stench of the Mexican weed invaded his lungs. The chief sat down at his desk, leaned back, and flipped his cigarette butt out the window. Oblivious to the scuffling sound outside as urchins fought over the tobacco stub, the Mexican, saying nothing, started slapping his leg with his riding crop.

The three men studied the chief idly in silence, the slapping of the riding crop a nerve-wracking strum on Ormsby's taut mental strings. And then the chief looked toward the door as the rapid staccato of boot heels issued from the outside corridor. Two local policemen, flanking a tall, handsomely dressed Mexican, entered the office. The escorted Mexican grazed on the faces of the men in the room with his eyes, then turned them on the police chief. There seemed to be no sign of fear or fright in the large brown orbs.

"Gentlemen," said the police chief, not interrupting the slapping of his riding crop, "may I introduce you to the man you've been seeking. Please meet El Zorro."

Chapter Nine

The handsome Mexican nicknamed El Zorro drew himself up and bowed to the strangers in the Mexicali police chief's office. "That is true. I am El Zorro." The words came out in fluent English, with scarcely a Latin accent. "What can I do for you, gentlemen?"

The men studied the dapper Mexican as he shot his cuffs and stared insouciantly at the assemblage. He had a slim, muscular build that gracefully transported a head with a thrusting jaw and large, dark eyes. It was easy to see why a woman could be lured into this Latino's four-poster.

Captain Fox was the first to regain his composure. "We're looking for a woman named Lyda Meyer. An American."

"May I ask why?" The tall Mexican thrust long fingers into his coat pocket to produce a pack of American cigarettes.

"She's wanted back in the States for murder. We know that you were with her in Los Angeles, and we trailed you south. We understand she's with you now."

A spark came into El Zorro's eyes as he flashed his cigarette pack around. There were no takers. Ormsby was happy to see that at least El Zorro was not going to further foul the air with the stench of Mexican tobacco. "Murder?" he asked, lifting his eyebrows.

"Murder," said Ormsby. "Maybe several."

The Mexican lit a Camel, took a deep drag. "I knew a girl back in L.A. named Edith Eva Meyer. At least that's what she called herself. I don't know if it's the woman you are seeking. Can you describe her?"

Ormsby stood, pulled Lyda's picture from his inside coat pocket, and handed it to El Zorro. The Mexican took it, studied it through eyes squinting from the smoke of the cigarette dangling from his lips. Ormsby's breath locked in his chest as he waited for the man's answer.

"Yes," he said quietly. "That is the woman who calls herself Edith Eva Meyer."

"Where is she now?" asked Ormsby, the words squeaking around the heart that had flopped into his mouth.

El Zorro shrugged his broad shoulders, presented his palms to the ceiling. "She's no longer with me. The day I left for Mexicali she went back to San Pedro."

"San Pedro!" said Captain Fox, coming to his feet.

"San Pedro," said the Mexican, obviously enjoying the center of attention. "She used to work at a cafe there. She decided to go back. She told me to write her there. As far as I know, she's there now."

For nearly an hour, the lawmen grilled the disarming Mexican, but were unable to shake his story. Finally, after extracting the address of the San Pedro cafe where Lyda might be working, the inquisitors thanked him for his cooperation and allowed him to leave.

As the echo of his steel-capped heels faded down the hall, Captain Fox turned to the Mexican chief. "Do you think our man is telling the truth?"

"I think so," said the chief. "If he had an American woman with him, we would have known about it. And El Zorro is no fool. He would not cover up for any woman who is wanted on a murder charge. He is too slick for that."

"Okay, Chief," said Fox. "We're off to San Pedro." He thanked the law officer for his help, then the three men picked up their hats and departed.

Orsmby, Fox, and Nolan felt the need for a hot bath and a good night's sleep. They spent the night at a hotel in Calexico, California. Refreshed, the men got an early start the next morning for Los Angeles, to complete the circle of their travels down south.

The results of their trip were not overwhelming, but at least they had emerged with a hot clue as to Lyda Meyer's whereabouts. They paused at Los Angeles only long enough to gas up, then proceeded on to San Pedro.

Ormsby was pensive during the last part of the journey, his mind preoccupied with the events of the last couple days. He was hopeful that his visit to the San Pedro cafe would bear fruit. He remembered the remark made by Lyda's girl friend from Boise, that Lyda liked sailors. If that were true, El Zorro's tip just might be valid, for San Pedro was awash in sailors from the San Pedro Naval Station.

But his hopes for the capture of the elusive fugitive had been crushed so many times, he hardly dared to be optimistic. He was in the doghouse with his wife at home, and the Twin Falls sheriff's office was less than enthusiastic about his romping around the world at taxpayer's expense. He had to produce some results or he was going to be in deep sheep dip. Little wonder Orsmby was in less than an euphoric mood as they entered San Pedro.

Making a courtesy call at the San Pedro police station, the men were given a map showing where the cafe was that had been mentioned by El Zorro. It proved to be down by the waterfront. While Ormsby navigated with the map, Captain Fox steered the dusty touring car toward the ocean. Finally spotting the cafe, Fox parked nearby, and the men disembarked. The fleet was in, and the streets were crowded with sailors.

As they walked into the dimly lit eatery, Ormsby made a quick survey of the place. Several waitresses in dowdy uniforms waited on tables. His eyes adjusting to the gloom, they went from one waitress to another. And then Orsmby again felt that sinking sensation. None of the waitresses resembled Lyda Meyer.

Ormsby joined Captain Fox, who was introducing himself to a man, obviously the proprietor, sitting at the cashier's counter. After identifying himself and flashing his badge, Fox asked, "Have you got a girl working here named Lyda Meyer?"

The proprietor thought for a moment. "Lyda? Doesn't ring a bell."

"How about Edith?" asked Ormsby. "Edith Meyer. She might have used that name."

"Edith! Now that does ring a bell. She used to work here."

"Used to?" Ormsby's voice dripped disappointment.

"Yes. She worked here for a while last year. Then went away. About ten days ago she came back, asked for her mail, and went away again. I don't know where she is now. She didn't leave a forwarding address."

Fox butted in. "How about your waitresses? She must have made a friend of at least one of them. Do you know if she was close to any of your girls?"

The proprietor closed his eyes in thought for a moment, and then said, "Wait a minute. Got an idea." He came from behind the counter and walked over to one of the employees. After a low conversation, the proprietor returned with the waitress in tow.

Not waiting for an introduction, Ormsby met the two with Lyda's picture in hand. "Is this the woman who used to work here?"

The two nodded in unison. "That's her," said the waitress. "That's Edith Meyer. I used to know her quite well. We roomed together for a while."

Once again Ormsby found his heart thumping. "Do you know where we might find her?"

The waitress looked up and flashed heavily mascaraed eyes at the deputy sheriff. "I'm afraid I don't, sir."

"Think hard. Anything at all you can tell us about this woman?"

"She was a good waitress," said the boss. "Had a nice way with the customers. The sailors especially. They always wanted to be waited on by Edith."

"Wait a minute," said the waitress, tapping long fingernails on the counter. "I remember something that might be helpful." She paused.

"For God's sake, woman, let's have it," said Ormsby.

"Yes. Just before she gave up her job here, Edith told me a secret." Again the waitress looked up with questioning eyes. "I hate to divulge a secret."

"For God's sake, divulge!" said Ormsby. "This woman is wanted for murder."

"Oh, mercy me!" Her hands fluttered to her mouth. "Did you say murder?"

"Murder."

"It can't be."

"It can be. It is. Your Edith is better known as Lyda Meyer. A very dangerous woman!"

"Oh, mercy me!" She looked over at the proprietor. "In that case, maybe it would be all right to betray a confidence."

"Under the circumstances," agreed the proprietor, "I think it might."

"Very well, then." She turned to Ormsby. "Edith told me in all secrecy that she might marry a petty officer in the navy."

Ormsby could only stare at the waitress, his mouth turning dry. "A petty officer?"

She nodded. "He was a real cute sailor."

Oh, God! Ormsby's mind reeled. Not another husband.

"He used to come here quite often," continued the waitress. "That's how they met. It was love at first sight."

"Lyda has had a lot of loves at first sight," said Fox. "Do you know this sailor's name?"

"Yes. His name was Southard. Nice looking gent. Had bedroom eyes."

"Other than having bedroom eyes," said Ormsby, "what else can you tell us about this Southard?"

"Well, when Edith came back here the other day for her mail, she told me Southard had been transferred to Honolulu. She said she was going to join him there. And they were to be married before he went to his new post."

"Oh, Jesus!" Ormsby wiped his face with the palm of his hand.

"Anything else you can tell us?"

"I'm afraid that's it." She blinked her large eyes at Ormsby. "I hope I've been of some help."

"You have, honey," said Captain Fox, reaching for his wallet. He pressed a dollar bill into her hand. "Most helpful."

"Gee!" she stuffed the bill into her apron. "You folks come back, ya hear?"

As the three men turned to walk out, she called after them. "Can you tell me how Edith might have murdered someone?"

"She's got a small problem," shot back Ormsby, as they went out the door. "She likes to poison people."

As this registered, the waitress released a little squawk, her mind racing back to the room she had shared and the meals she had eaten with Edith—Lyda—Meyer. "Oh, mercy me!" came words muffled by the balled fists at her mouth.

The commander of the San Pedro Navy Yard was a bullnecked mountain of a man who looked as though he could chew rivets and spit battleships. Their badges ushered the three lawmen through the military channels and into the admiral's presence. Speaking for the three men, Captain Fox explained their mission. Not one for pleasantries, the commander said little, but summoned his aide to guide the men to the office of the director of personnel.

Here, yet another briefing was given by Fox to a tall, pipe-smoking captain who served as personnel director for the San Pedro Navy Command. The officer listened attentively to the detective, then directed one of his clerks to retrieve the file of Paul Southard. Minutes that seemed like eons dragged by, underscored by the gurgling of the captain's pipe constantly being stoked by large kitchen matches. Finally the clerk returned with a thick personnel file. The captain scanned it quickly, then recapped the information.

"It appears that Edith Eva Meyer and Vincent Paul Southard, chief petty officer on the U.S.S. *Monterey*, were married in Los Angeles on November 28, 1920. The bride gave her occupation as nurse. Shortly after the wedding, Southard was transferred to Pearl Harbor, Hawaii. Mrs. Southard followed him there just recently."

Ormsby found himself almost numb as these words sunk in. He could only blink his eyes at the captain.

"God damn!" expounded Detective Fox, banging his fist on the captain's desk. "We're cornering our quarry. Now we have our work cut out for us. Nolan, you check out the marriage license. Ormsby, cable the Honolulu police and ask them to nab Lyda. Then have your Twin Falls authorities cable a warrant to Hawaii charging her with murder. The Hawaiians won't be able to hold her long without a warrant."

Ormsby came to his senses, nodding to acknowledge Fox's orders.

A broad grin split the detective's features as he thrust out his hand to the naval officer. "Many thanks for all your help, Captain." He turned to his cohorts. "Come on, men, let's get cracking before Lyda ducks out of Honolulu."

As Fox headed for the door, the navy man called after him. "Detective Fox, you're pretty good at giving orders."

Fox ushered his colleagues out the door, then putting on his hat, grinned back at the captain. "Sometimes I'm inclined to get a little bossy."

The officer fired another match to his percolater and leaned back in his chair. "If you ever need a job, give me a call. The navy needs men like you."

Fox grunted as he went out the door. "You kidding? And miss all this fun?"

The three men returned to Los Angeles to make Captain Fox's office their command post. A check with the marriage license bureau records confirmed that the wedding of Edith Eva Meyer and CPO Vincent Paul Southard had, indeed, taken place on the twenty-eighth of November.

Ormsby had cabled the Honolulu police headquarters, asking that the comely redhead who had tacked on yet another surname be taken into custody. He then wired Sheriff Sherman in Twin Falls, asking him to expedite the cable warrant to the Honolulu chief of police. There was nothing to do now but wait.

Ormsby sat in a straight chair, leaning back against the wall. As he nervously lit a fresh cigarette from the butt of his old, he ruminated on recent events that were transpiring almost too rapidly. Scenes flashed across his mind like a spinning kaleidoscope. What if Lyda had gotten wind of the investigation and had fled Hawaii, slipping through the net like she had so many times before?

The port authorities were no help in determining if the fugitive had even actually boarded the boat. Furthermore, her name had not been on any ship's manifest. This was not surprising, as Lyda could have used an alias to throw her pursuers off the scent. Or maybe she hadn't even taken the boat, and had gone into hiding somewhere in the States.

Ormsby's eyes burned from lack of sleep, his lids feeling like sandpaper as they lowered over his orbs. He was tired. Tired of traveling. Tired of frustrations. Tired of dirty clothes he hadn't had time to launder. As he waited, stuporous, for a message from Honolulu, he mashed his cigarette butt into a nearby ashtray and lit another one.

Deputy Sheriff Ormsby's message to the Honolulu Police Department ended up on the cluttered desk of the captain of detectives, Arthur McDuffie. Figuring the pursuit of a pretty woman would be a lot more rewarding than trying to track down the tourists, pimps, prostitutes, and gangsters who kept coming up missing in his territory, McDuffie threw the cable on top of the pile and went into action.

His first call to the Pearl Harbor naval headquarters had confirmed the fact that a Mrs. Southard had reached the island a short time ago. Chief Petty Officer Southard's ship, the *Monterey*, was in harbor, and the newlyweds had taken up residence in an apartment at Vineyard and Fort streets.

A grin made a rare appearance below McDuffie's thick mustache as he hung up the phone. He knew the area well where the Southards had taken up housekeeping. Capturing this notorious refugee should be a snap. He put on his hat, pulled the brim down over his eyes, and headed for the door.

At Vineyard and Fort streets, McDuffie found an apartment building. Near the front door was a list of the building's occupants. Tracing down the list with his forefinger, his eyes suddenly flared. The name Paul Southard leaped out at him. Captain McDuffie pushed the button beside the name. He waited patiently, and then there was a click as the vestibule door opened.

McDuffie almost sauntered as he went up the stairs, his coat unbuttoned to give ready access to his holstered gun. Reaching the second-story landing, he looked around in the darkened corridor. At the far end of the hall a door opened. Standing in the doorway was a woman.

McDuffie strode toward the open door, his eyes adjusting to the dark hall. As he came closer, he focused on a full-figured young lady wearing a pink housedress. A pair of wide, blue eyes were surveying him questioningly. "Yes?"

"Are you Mrs. Paul Southard?" The detective smiled disarmingly.

"Why, yes." The words were soft, melodious, as the woman returned his smile.

The captain was now facing her. He suddenly had misgivings as he appraised the comely young lady. Highlighted by the light coming from the room behind her, her red hair glowed in a soft halo. He buttoned his coat. There would be no need for his holstered firearm. This was his kind of felon. His mind spun back to the collection of child-fondlers, muggers, and rapists whose reports littered his desk. One thing about Twin Falls, Idaho. They sure knew how to wrap a murderer up into a pretty package.

"I am Detective Arthur McDuffie. Of the Honolulu Police Department." He flashed his badge, continuing in a courteous tone. "I have a warrant for your arrest. I'm afraid you'll have to come down to police headquarters with me."

These casual words had the effect of a bombshell on the woman. Her pretty face contorted and turned white. She stepped back as if to duck into her apartment and slam the door on the detective's face. And then, as suddenly, her demeanor changed again. "I'm sure there must be some mistake."

"No mistake, ma'am."

"Well," she said, tossing her head defiantly. "Let me get my things. We'll go down to your office and straighten out this ridiculous misunderstanding."

"I'd appreciate that, ma'am."

As he followed her into the apartment, she turned to him. "Will I have time to change my clothes? I'm in a housedress."

"I'm afraid not, Mrs. Southard. You look just fine."

"I don't really. My hair's a mess."

"It looks just fine."

"Then I'll get my coat." She reached into the clothes closet and pulled out a fur coat. She handed it to the policeman, turning her back so he could help her put it on.

As he did, he got a whiff of her perfume. He fumbled with her coat as she tried to find its sleeves. It was little wonder this woman had no problem luring men into wedlock. He took another deep sniff, his eyes almost closing. There was no question about it. Lyda Southard was his kind of murderer. Reluctantly, his mind returned to the business at hand. "I don't think you're really going to need this fur coat, ma'am. It's a muggy eighty degrees outside."

"A woman should look nice in public. And since you won't give me time to change, this will have to do." She wrapped the coat around her, picked up her purse, and headed for the door. They went out of the room, Lyda locked the door with the key from her purse, and McDuffie fell into step beside her as they headed down the hall.

"I'm sure, Captain, you are aware of the penalties for a false arrest."

McDuffie fought the urge to take her hand. "Yes, ma'am. I'm aware."

Chapter Ten

Deputy Sheriff Virgil Ormsby stretched like a contented cat, luxuriating in the soft bed. God, it was good to be home. In his own bed. That didn't smell like tobacco smoke, and had clean sheets, and no hotel bedbugs. He didn't care if he ever hit the road again.

He looked over at his wife, who was sleeping soundly on her back. He loved to watch her in the early morning as she slept, her soft snoring more like the purr of a kitten. Breathing shallowly, she took in air, exhaled in little puffs through slightly parted lips.

He was tempted to kiss her wide, sensuous mouth. Instead, he carefully folded down the comforter, exposing the top of her negligee. She generally slept in a nightgown, but in honor of his homecoming she had slipped on the filmy peignoir he had brought her from Mexico. Gently he slid down the shoulder strap to expose a creamy breast. He sighed deeply. Whatever shortcomings his wife might have, they were not in the bosom department. She had full, firm breasts that even when she was lying on her back stood up proud, pointing to the ceiling.

He lay quietly, watching her chest responding to the slight rise and fall of her breathing. His thoughts went back to the previous day when he had arrived home from Los Angeles. He had been met with a very cool reception. Nellie had made a scene, reiterating the fact that she was definitely not going to stay married to a gypsy. He comforted her as best he could, explaining the mission, the long, arduous chase that had turned up so many frustrations, and the final victory of Lyda's apprehension in Hawaii.

Confirming his undying love by showering her with gifts he had brought from Mexico, and vowing to curtail further chases around the country tracking down winsome redheads, he finally won her over. After all, they decided, they were deeply in love, and it was Nellie's missing him so much that had created the testy conduct on her part. With a meeting of minds, it was only logical that a meeting of bodies should follow, and they lost no time diving into the eiderdown. Nellie's new negligee spent most of the night at the foot of the bed.

Ormsby reached out with his forefinger and softly traced the outline of her nipple. After a moment of this, a soft sigh issued from her, and she slowly blinked her eyes open. She looked at her husband, sleepily put her arm around his neck and pulled his head to her bosom. He kissed the curvature of her breast as she sighed. "The only thing nice about having you gone so long is that it's so much fun making up for lost time when you get home."

"It is at that." He touched her firming nipple with the tip of his tongue, his hands circling her waist.

"Oh, Virgil, I love you so."

"And I love you, Lyda. With all my heart."

Even before he realized what he had said, he felt her body stiffen. "Say that again?"

"Oh, my God!"

"You called me Lyda!"

He looked into her face. "My God, honey, it was a slip. I've had her on my mind so much lately — "

"You called me *Lyda!* You were just about to make love to me, and you called me *Lyda!*"

Orsmby could have bitten his tongue off. "Honey, she means nothing to me. You know that. It's you I love."

"You will kindly get your hands off of me." She separated from him, yanking up the strap of her negligee. "And you will kindly get out of my bed."

"Honey! You've got to understand — "

"Oh, I understand all right. You have become obsessed with this woman. Even when you profess your love to me, you call me by that woman's name. I want you out of my bedroom. I want you out of my house. Now!"

Massaging his aching back, Ormsby presented himself to Sheriff Sherman, who had just returned from a trip. His boss looked up from the paperwork on his desk and fixed his deputy with a look accompanied by a large grin. "So how did you sleep last night, Val?"

Ormsby traded rubbing for scratching. "We've got to do something about the mattresses in our jail. I think we also have fleas."

Sherman grunted. "You're lucky we had an empty cell. Or you might have had an interesting roommate."

"Yeah. I'm shot in the ass with luck." He scratched his head. "You ever slept in your own jail?"

"Can't say as I have."

"Try it sometime. Maybe if we made some improvements, we'd attract a better class of people."

"We'll give it some thought."

"Do that. You ever been kicked out of your own house?"

"No. You want to tell me about it?"

"No." Ormsby plopped down in a chair in front of the sheriff's desk. "Besides, I think you pretty well know the story."

"I reckon I do. You've been away too long. When the cat's away, the mice get nervous."

Ormsby nodded. "Something like that. Anyway, I made one fatal mistake. I called my wife Lyda."

Sherman couldn't surpress a chuckle. "That was not too shrewd."

"God! I realized the second I said it that my goose was cooked. Nellie doesn't want to see me again."

Sherman's heart went out to his miserable deputy. "You're a good man, Val. You two will patch it up. In the meantime, I've got an assignment for you."

"Good. Maybe it'll take my mind off my troubles."

"It should. Something about grass skirts and swaying palm trees that makes a man forget his problems."

Ormsby stopped in mid-scratch to stare at his boss. "I'm not sure I follow."

"It's simple. Your favorite fugitive is in a Hawaiian jail awaiting extradition. The lieutenant governor has signed the papers, and someone has to go to Hawaii and pick her up. Since you've done such a good job tracking her down, it's been agreed that you should be the one to go."

Ormsby's face brightened, and then he sagged in his chair. His initial reaction had been one of elation at visiting Hawaii, and more importantly, bringing in his long-sought quarry. But this euphoria had been quickly doused as his thoughts turned to his wife. His furrowed brow was not lost on his boss.

"What's the matter, Val? I thought you'd do handstands at the prospect of an all-expense-paid trip to the land of natives who like to dance in grass skirts and shake their coconuts — "

"Thanks, Chief. For the opportunity. But it'll shoot a month by the time a boat gets to Hawaii and back. Being gone that long is all I need to really put the cap on my marital problems. Nellie will leave me for sure."

Sherman leaned back in his chair, feeling a pang of sympathy for his hardworking deputy. "I anticipated this might be a problem, Val. So I've come up with an idea. I think you might like it. Had a little trouble getting it approved topside, but we prevailed."

Ormsby stared blankly at his boss. "I have no idea what you're talking about, but if you can spread a little oil on my turbulent domestic waters, you sure got my vote."

"Good. Now get a good grip on your galluses. Here's the plan."

Deputy Sheriff Virgil Ormsby had a little trouble getting through the front door of his house. Finally, his wife said he could come in long enough to pack his belongings so he could move out of her life forever. Ormsby went into the bedroom, started packing his clothes. Nellie stood by the door, her arms laced over her chest, watching the proceedings through swollen eyes. She wiped away a tear from her cheek and asked, "Where will you go?"

"I'm off to Hawaii."

She sniffed. "Did you say . . . Hawaii?"

"Hawaii. It's a little island quite a ways west of here."

"I know where it is. Of course you're going to Hawaii. Why wouldn't my globe-trotting husband be going off to Hawaii? Leaving his wife home alone for months on end."

"Weeks on end," he said, trying to fold a starched shirt as he stuffed his clothes into his Gladstone bag.

"Can you blame me for leaving you, Virgil?"

"Yes. Yes, Nellie, I can."

She wiped her nose with a handkerchief from her apron. "Not only are you gone all the time, but when you are home you are completely obsessed by another woman."

"Only in a professional way. Not in a sexual way."

"It doesn't matter. She has taken over our lives. And you let her."

"There is only one way to cure you of this obsession you have over my obsession."

"And just what is that?"

"You are going to meet this woman who has come between us. Face to face. You are going to see, first-hand, the woman who is ruining our marriage. By confronting this imagined specter, you will slay your incubus, and come to grips with your fears. Then, and only then, can we get our marriage back on track."

She blew her nose. "That is not the way to fold a shirt."

"Then come over here and show me."

"No." She was obviously having problems with her resolve. "And just when am I going to come face to face with this monster?"

"Very soon. Start packing."

"Start what?"

"Packing. We're going to Hawaii."

She grabbed the doorknob for support. "Did I hear you say *we're* going to Hawaii?"

"That's what I said. Now quit standing there blowing your nose, and start packing."

"I don't understand."

"It's very simple. Sheriff Sherman kicked me out of his jail. And when I told him you wouldn't let me come home, he said he'd fix it. And he did. Don't forget to pack your bathing suit."

"We can't afford my ticket to Hawaii." Her resolve was crumbling fast. "Even if I consented to go with you."

"No problem. We are going at taxpayer's expense. I will go on official business, to pick up Lyda. You will go with me as a deputy."

"A *what?*"

"A deputy. Sheriff Sherman came up with the plan. You will be sworn in today."

"Gracious sakes! I don't know anything about deputying."

"All you have to do is what you're told by the deputy sheriff. That's me. Now I'm telling you to start packing."

"Merciful heavens!" Her brain spinning, she chewed on her lower lip. "How could you possibly justify my going at the county's expense?"

"Very simple. We are picking up a female felon who is very dangerous. When we pick her up, someone has to be with her at all times. Even when she takes a shower or goes to the bathroom. Since men aren't supposed to accompany women into the ladies' room, it's obvious that a female must be along to keep an eye on her. Since we have no females in the sheriff's department, we have to deputize one. You are the lucky deputee."

"I see. You want me to go along and wet nurse a very dangerous woman who has killed half a dozen husbands."

"Probably more than that. That's only the ones we know about."

"Oh, fine."

"I'm not a bit worried about your safety. Lyda Southard, in spite of her reputation, is no match for a certain young lady I know." He looked at his wife out of the corner of his eye. "I won't mention any names, but she has quite a temper."

A slight smile broke through the overcast. "I guess I do have an Irish streak in me."

"You might say that. Well, are you going to start packing?"

She mulled this a moment, looking longingly at her husband. "Yes. I have always wanted to see Hawaii. And the woman who has taken my husband from me. I don't care if she's Jack the Ripper, I'm going to Hawaii and bring her back."

"That's my girl."

She shook her head in disbelief. "Imagine. Going to Hawaii."

"On an all-expense-paid trip."

"This is too good to be true." Nellie stepped out of the ashes of her resolve, flung herself into her husband's arms. "I'm going to kiss Sheriff Sherman."

"You have to go through channels. You may start with the deputy sheriff."

She did.

Nellie W. Ormsby was sworn in as deputy two days before leaving for San Francisco. She carried with her extradition papers signed by C. C. Moore, the lieutenant governor of Idaho. On May 18, 1921, the Ormsbys sailed for Hawaii on the ocean liner *Matsonia* to bring back Lyda Trueblood-Dooley-McHaffie-Lewis-Meyer-Southard, charged with murder.

Nellie was well educated, but her travels to date had barely exceeded the boundaries of Idaho. Her honeymoon with Virgil at Lava Hot Springs had been wonderful, but this ocean cruise was something she had only dreamed of. As she was wined, dined, and catered to on the stately liner, her animosity toward her husband completely dissolved in the wake that fantailed from the stern of the ship. She was having a marvelous time.

Ormsby was also enjoying the trip, it being his first time to really relax since he had embarked on his odyssey. He was especially pleased that his marriage was back on track. Once again Nellie was the pretty, loving spouse he had fallen in love with years ago. But in spite of his stomach being bulged by the excellent cuisine on the ship, and his every whim being catered to by his own personal steward, he still had a few nagging problems.

His work was not over. And it wouldn't be until Lyda was back in Twin Falls, safely behind bars. And then another thought began to plague him. What if Lyda committed suicide? It would be just like her to thwart his victory in successfully tracking her down. The more he thought about it, the more worried he became. He finally hunted out the ship's radio room and fired a cable off to Captain McDuffie, the Honolulu detective chief, requesting that he take every precaution against the possibility of Lyda taking her own life.

This done, he felt a little better.

As the *Matsonia* plowed leisurely across the Pacific toward the

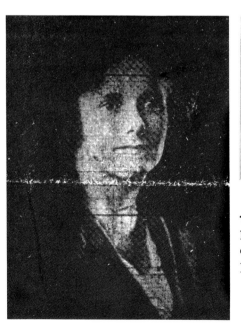

The many faces of Lyda. Top left, as a young lady. Top right, at the time of her first capture. Lower left, San Francisco police photo. Above, awaiting her trial.

The Blue Lakes ranch house, a few miles from Twin Falls, Idaho, where Ed Meyer was foreman until his mysterious death.

Alfonso Dooley, seated, whose two sons were victims of Lady Bluebeard.

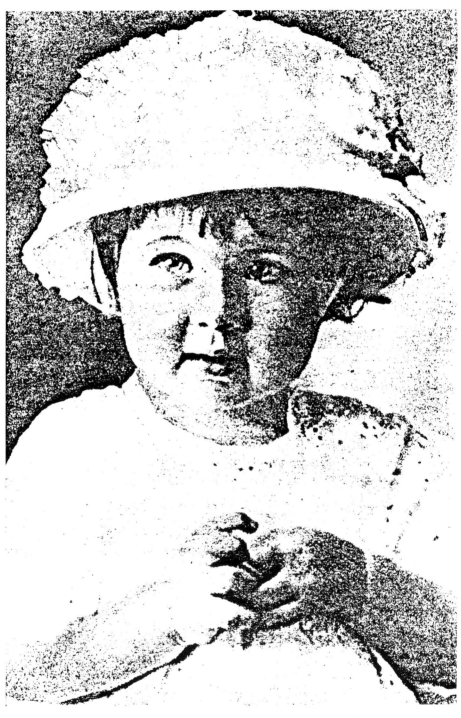

Laura Marie Dooley, Lyda's pretty three-year-old daughter by her first marriage, who, like her father and uncle, died under mysterious circumstances.

First "Mrs. Bluebeard" Talk to Chronicle
Her Only Thought Is to See Her Mother

Mrs. Lyda Southard,
Arrested in Honolulu

Deputy Sheriff V. H. Ormsby
of Twin Falls, Idaho

San Francisco Chronicle photo of Lyda Southard, in the custody of Deputy Sheriff V. H. Ormsby, arriving in San Francisco en route to Twin Falls, Idaho.

Lyda with her captor, Deputy Sheriff Val Ormsby, left, and Sheriff E. R. Sherman.

Deputy Sheriff Val Ormsby, who relentlessly tracked Lyda down.

E. R. Sherman, sheriff of Twin Falls County, who as Deputy Sheriff Val Ormsby's boss played a pivotal role in Lyda's apprehension.

The adversaries: Above, for the state, County Prosecutor Frank L. Stephan, lawyer E. A. Wallers, and Attorney General Roy L. Black. Below, for the defense, consulting with Lyda are lawyers W. P. Guthrie, Homer Mills, A. R. Hicks, and A. J. Meyers.

$50-Reward-$50
MRS. LYDA SOUTHARD
No. 3052

Escaped from the Idaho State Penitentiary, Boise, Idaho, on the night of May 4th, 1931.

Received at the Penitentiary on November 9th, 1921, from Twin Falls County. Charge, murder in the second degree. Term, 10 years to life.

DESCRIPTION: American, white; age 39; height 5 feet 2 inches; weight 142 pounds; hair light brown; eyes blue with brown iris; complexion sallow. Bobbed hair.

MARKS AND PECULIARITIES: Has very shifty look, small features.

FINGER PRINT FORMULA: 27   IM   19
                                    28   OI   17

BERTILLON: 17-4; 14-2; 9-6; 22-4; 40-1; 57-1

Fifty Dollars Reward will be paid for her capture and will extradite from any point in the United States or Canada.

ARREST AND WIRE

R. E. THOMAS, Warden

Idaho State Penitentiary   BOISE. IDAHO

This reward poster was circulated all over the western states following Lyda's break from prison.

Harlan Lewis, Lyda's third husband, who became a victim of her apple pie.

Lyda with her fifth husband, Paul Southard, one of the few who escaped her deadly web.

The twelve good men and true who decided Lyda Southard's fate during her long criminal trial.

LADDER THAT HELPED LYDA TO FREEDOM

OUTSIDE AFTER 10 LONG YEARS

Newspaper photos of the prison wall that Lyda scaled on the night of May 4, 1931, by joining two iron rose trellises to make a ladder. She then slid down a rope of twisted blankets to freedom.

Lyda Southard Blunders Into Hands Of Waiting Police at Topeka, Kan.; Warden Leaves Today to Get Woman

Principals of Thrilling Escape

Newspaper photos of David Minton, left, who helped Lyda escape from prison, and Lyda herself, right, that appeared shortly after Minton's confession led police to Lyda in Topeka, Kansas.

Idaho's Dames of Fame

By Sylvia Johnson Wood

Widow Lyda Used Poison For Seasoning

Lyda Southard, Idaho ranch wife, had buried her fourth husband in 1921 when the Twin Falls authorities began to feel that coincidence was being stretched a mite too far when it came to combining ptomaine poisoning with life insurance policies. By the time the police caught up with the perennial widow in Honolulu, she had one, possibly two, more check marks on the poison bottle . . . and was married for the fifth time.

Convicted by an Idaho jury of second degree murder, Mrs. Southard was sentenced to from 10 years to life in the state penitentiary. The 10 year limit was prophetic. Just after that length of time had passed, she went over the wall, literally, with the aid of a rose trellis, a garden hose and a susceptible fellow convict. By the time the law again caught up with her, in the middle west, she had annexed a sixth husband and was tenderly urging him to take out a $20,000 insurance policy.

Returned to the Idaho penitentiary, she took her incarceration philosophically.

"Drop around and see me

GRAVE-EYED Mrs. Southard "Mugged" by Prison Photographer When She Began Her Fourteen-Year Sentence.

LYDA SOUTHARD . . . married 'em and buried 'em.

when I get out, boys," she used to say to the guards. "I'll bake you up a bunch of biscuits." In 1942 the pardon board, feeling that her girlish charm had faded enough to remove her from the "femme fatale" category, granted her a full pardon.

The tabloids had a field day with Lyda's exploits.

flyspecks on the navigational charts known as the Hawaiian group, Captain McDuffie was not without his problems in Honolulu.

He had properly incarcerated the temptress in the Honolulu jail, placing her in the custody of a shrewd, disarming matron named Mrs. Ah Fam. Mrs. Ah Fam's cunning was perpetually masked by a large grin that nearly joined her ears. Acknowledging the cable from Deputy Sheriff Ormsby, McDuffie promptly had the matron strip-search her ward. Mrs. Ah Fam examined every nook and cavity in Lyda's body that might conceal any kind of instrument that could be used to snuff out her own life. Finding nothing, a twenty-four-hour watch was established to assure the prisoner's safety.

In the meantime, Captain McDuffie had launched his own investigation. With the help of the Pearl Harbor naval authorities, he located Lyda's current husband, Chief Petty Officer Paul Vincent Southard, aboard his ship the U.S.S. *Monterey*, moored in Pearl Harbor.

The handsome young newlywed was completely decked by the news about his wife. He steadfastly refused to believe that his loved one was involved in the mysterious deaths of a number of husbands. "The charge is absolutely ridiculous," the sailor told McDuffie in the wardroom of his ship. "There is no sweeter, more loving, or more beautiful woman on the face of this earth. That's why I married her."

In spite of his case-hardened demeanor, inside McDuffie felt a pang of sympathy for the shocked sailor. But he had to get on with his investigation. "Did you ever take out an insurance policy in your wife's favor?"

"Certainly not."

"Are you sure?"

"Positive. We've only been married a short while."

"Your wife has been known to act very fast."

"Why, you son of a bitch!"

McDuffie saw the blood boiling in the eyes of the seaman, and for a moment he thought the man was going to haul off and punch him. "Easy, son. I'm just doing my duty."

"Well, sir, I'd be obliged if you'd take your duty someplace else. You're barking up the wrong tree." Southard unclenched his fists. "How dare you make these accusations against my wife!"

"Sorry to upset you, son. As I said, I'm just doing my job."

"You'd oblige me, sir, by getting the hell off of my ship."

McDuffie grimaced, picked up his hat and headed through the door of the wardroom. "I'll be in touch, sailor."

Continuing his research, Detective McDuffie unearthed some unsettling information concerning the young sailor. Chief Petty Officer Southard was obviously trying to shield his new bride. Checking with Southard's commanding officer, McDuffie was furnished the information that the seaman had, indeed, applied to the navy for a ten-thousand-dollar government insurance policy. This application had been rejected, due to legal complications.

McDuffie assigned his men to canvass the Honolulu insurance companies, and one of them hit pay dirt when he found a local company that had an application pending for a five-thousand-dollar policy. Its beneficiary: Mrs. Lyda Southard.

When confronted with this information, Southard finally admitted to submitting the applications, but maintained vehemently that his wife had not suggested the insurance. The whole idea, he insisted stoutly, had been his own.

In the meantime, Lyda Southard paced the floor of her barred cubicle. She maintained that the prison food was not agreeing with her, and she was sick. Mrs. Ah Fam called in the prison doctor, who found nothing wrong with her.

As the matron gained her confidence, Lyda confided in her that she was glad she was returning to Twin Falls. She welcomed the chance to fight the charges against her.

Mrs. Ah Fam smiled and patted her hand.

Chief Petty Officer Southard moved into the Leonard Hotel on the morning his wife was arrested so he could be near her. Although territorial law could hold Lyda only for a short time, she voluntarily stayed in jail. Sheriff Charles Rose said she was given better treatment because she was staying voluntarily.

Apparently the cable from Twin Falls charging her with murder was slow to arrive, because on May 15 Lyda issued a statement to the press. It was printed in the *Honolulu Advertiser* on that date:

I have been informed that under the laws of the territory of Hawaii, I cannot be detained over 48 hours without a criminal charge against me. I do not wish to take advantage of this provision of the law and do not wish or care to have a criminal charge of any kind placed against me. I am willing to stay and be detained right in the city jail until I am ready to go to the mainland in charge of any official who might be sent for me.

I waive all rights that I may have for damages against Mr. Arthur McDuffie and against all other officials of Honolulu. I will not permit any attorney to intercede in my behalf for contesting my extradition. I wish to state that the treatment accorded me in jail has been considerate and courteous.

According to the Honolulu paper, attorneys speculated that Lyda was staying in jail to lay a foundation for an insanity plea. Lyda turned down offers as high as $250 from island papers for a statement as to her guilt or innocence.

On the same date, her husband, Paul Southard, issued a companion statement to the press:

> My wife is in a seriously weakened condition through confinement and lack of nourishment at the county jail. If she is to have the strength to make the trip to the mainland she should be allowed to leave the jail in the custody of Sheriff Ormsby or his wife or myself until her departure.
>
> She is willing to go back and face her accusers and says she is innocent. I firmly believe in her innocence and believe that in the end she will be acquitted. She is a victim of circumstance and I know that innocent persons are not made to suffer in America. Her condition is not due to a hunger strike or a guilty conscience.

One of the few times Lyda spoke in the Honolulu jail was when she asked Captain Arthur McDuffie about the evidence against her.

"What kind of poison do they say I used?" she asked.

"The kind you kill weeds with."

"They'll have to prove that," she said.

Complaining of ill health, Lyda was moved to the jail's hospital annex under the care of Dr. R. G. Ayer. Ayer reported that Lyda was very nervous but not seriously ill. Because of her condition, Captain McDuffie ordered the prison staff not to let Lyda see a newspaper report that stated her parents would not support her.

Also kept from the woman was an article in the *Salt Lake Telegram* that quoted Val Ormsby:

> Lyda used her charm as a business asset. She swept the men of her choice off their feet — courted them so persistently they could not escape.
>
> Take poor Ed Meyer for example. She rigged herself out fit to kill, bought a long mink coat and a closed car. Everybody in town was talking about how she ran around to dances. She talked around town that she wasn't in love with Ed, but she wanted a home and that some time she would learn to love him.

On May 24, the *Matsonia* steamed into Honolulu Harbor. From their vantage point on the forward deck, the Deputy Sheriffs Ormsby watched entranced as the beauties of the tropical island glided by.

On the dock awaiting the ship's arrival, Captain McDuffie watched impatiently as the big ocean liner neared and was finally tethered to its mooring cleats by sweating dockmen manhandling its huge hawsers. McDuffie did not like the hot sun, and his seersucker suit quickly became a wet rag as he continually removed his panama hat and wiped the perspiration from its sweatband.

Since McDuffie had never met Sheriff Ormsby and had no idea what he looked like, he had introduced himself to several couples coming down the gangplank before finally connecting with the Ormsbys.

"Damn, am I glad to see you!" said the detective, following introductions. "No offense, but I'll sure be glad to get your fugitive off my hands."

"Has she been a problem?" asked Ormsby.

"She's really been a boil on the ass of progress." McDuffie looked at Ormsby's wife. "Sorry, ma'am. I didn't mean to use that kind of language. I'm not used to being in the presence of a lady."

"That's quite all right, Captain," Nellie said smiling. "Lyda seems to have that effect on men."

Mr. and Mrs. Ormsby checked into a hotel near the beach. While Nellie unpacked their baggage, Ormsby accompanied Captain McDuffie to the jail. Their footsteps echoing hollowly through the corridor, the two men stopped before a dimly lit cell. It reeked of human odor magnified by the dankness of the high humidity. And then, peering into the gloom, Ormsby found himself staring into the face of Lyda Trueblood.

"Hello, Val Ormsby," came a low, sultry voice.

"Hello, Lyda." Ormsby's flat voice belied the emotions that were seething within him. Slowly adjusting to the darkness, his eyes took in the figure that was materializing before him. Lyda's red hair framed a face that had gotten a bit pudgy, but her blue eyes still exuded a sensuality that left little doubt as to why five husbands had been bewitched by her charms. She wore a simple flowered dress that adorned a figure slightly on the plump side, yet still well proportioned.

"You're looking well, Val."

"So are you, Lyda."

He stared at her silently, his mind racing back to the research he had done while pursuing his quarry, and to his own memories. Lyda had arrived with her folks from Missouri when she was in her early teens. The Truebloods had bought a farm near Twin Falls, where Lyda had graduated from high school. Studying the graduation pictures in the high school annual, Ormsby was taken by the attractive face that peered at him from its pages. She had been very popular in school, due in no small part to her extraordinary good looks, a bubbling personality, and a figure that summoned wolf whistles from the men in front of the cigar store. Ormsby had seen her around town and had gotten to know her casually.

And now, this comely woman, who had led him on a merry chase over thousands of miles, was smiling pleasantly at him through the bars of her cell, as if they had just met at a Twin Falls coffee shop. Could this truly be the woman who had dispatched numerous men in such a bizarre manner? As Ormsby stared at her, he suddenly realized that this confrontation seemed to have affected him much more than it had her.

"I understand you are taking me back to Twin Falls." Her words snapped him out of his reverie.

"Yes. We'll leave as soon as we get the paperwork finished."

"I'm so glad. I look forward to getting home. So we can have a trial and I can be acquitted of all these terrible things the papers are printing about me."

"I'm sure you'll have your day in court, Lyda."

"They tell me your wife is with you."

"Yes."

"Splendid. I've always wanted to meet her."

"And she has certainly wanted to meet you."

Chapter Eleven

Chief Petty Officer Paul Southard was not one to give up without a fight. On May 25, he told Captain McDuffie he intended to contest his wife's extradition.

Advised McDuffie, "The Hawaii Territory has never lost an extradition battle. You may as well save your money. It might come in handy to help in defending your wife at her trial."

Southard heeded the captain's advice.

On May 26, the Ormsbys and Capt. Arthur McDuffie took Lyda for her first drive since her incarceration. People on Iwilei Road, noticing McDuffie and figuring that Lyda was one of the women in the car, pointed and jeered. A mile or so of this and Lyda said she was sick and refused to go any farther.

The next day the same entourage headed for the Pali, but ended up only going several miles up Nuuanu Valley before aborting the mission.

On this date, Paul Southard entertained a lawyer's suggestion that he might not be legally married to Lyda. Indiana law required divorcees to wait two years before remarrying. Southard had divorced his first wife, who ran out on him, only six months before he married Lyda.

Southard told several reporters that he was willing to remarry Lyda in jail if necessary. However, City Attorney William Heen told him that territorial law would uphold such a marriage, but mainland courts would not.

On June 2, City Physician R. C. Ayer and naval hospital doctor

Joseph Schwartz examined Lyda and concluded she was neither physically ill nor a typhoid carrier. They certified she was ready to sail the following Wednesday.

As they prepared for departure, Lyda's father issued the following news release:

> Press reports saying we would not support our daughter are totally false. We stated that if we though she was guilty we would not support her. Since then there have been charges made that we know are false. We plan to support her.
>
> It looks as though certain individuals are working for publicity. Two at least are having a grand pleasure trip at the expense of the taxpayers and this girl's reputation. Now, I want to ask this of the good people of Twin Falls. That they withhold their verdict at least until the girl has had a hearing. All we ask is a square deal for the girl.

On June 1, Mr. and Mrs. Ormsby escorted Lyda Southard up the gangplank of the returning *Matsonia*. Paul Southard accompanied his wife, choosing to be with her until the last possible moment.

Deputy Sheriff Ormsby was fully aware of the national newspaper coverage that had attended Lyda since the results of the preliminary trial labeling her an ogress. Especially troubling were the tabloids, with their gruesome headlines heralding her latest exploits as the doings of "Lethal Lyda" or "The Arsenic Widow." Ormsby reluctantly found himself center stage as this chilling scenario unfolded.

He was uneasy with members of the Fourth Estate, and had dodged the many requests he had had for interviews. Even aware of all the press interest, however, he was hardly prepared for the throngs of curiosity-saters who showed up at the dock to see his notorious charge in person.

It was almost a festive occasion, Lyda acting like any lucky vacationer about to embark on an ocean cruise. Her neck was encircled with sweet-smelling leis made from the colorful petals of pikake, plumeria, and vanda orchids that had been bestowed on her by Mrs. Ah Fam, and her husband, in the traditional Hawaiian departure ritual. As they jostled through the crowd to the gangplank, several well-wishers added to the flowered garlands and tried to kiss Lyda in the aloha farewell. The Ormsbys were nervous until they got their ward safely up the gangplank, fearing God-only-knew-what act the morbid thrill-seekers might perform, just so they could pass on to their grandchildren the fact that they had actually seen — and maybe touched — the famous murderess.

A popular movie actress, also making her departure with her retinue of toadies, was utterly flabbergasted to find her spotlight had been completely stolen by a somewhat pudgy matron with leis up to her nose. Who was this strange woman posing demurely at the ship's rail for the photographers, who were stumbling all over themselves to record the woman's departure?

As the cameramen snapped away, Lyda gave the press a brief statement: "I am entirely innocent, and I look forward to the trip with optimism. I am anxious to get back to Twin Falls and face my accusers." Then she smiled beguilingly at the photographers, took off her hat, and threw her head back, allowing the shore breezes to comb her red hair.

The "all ashore" announcement was made. Lyda kissed her doting husband goodbye, smothering his vows that he would take leave and be with her at her trial. Then the gangplank was lifted, the stentorian blast of the horn reverberated throughout the ship, the harbor began to boil from the backwash of huge propellers, and the *Matsonia* started gliding majestically out to sea.

Lyda watched as the waving people on the dock shrank into the distance. Finally she stopped waving and stood immobile at the railing, staring out at the horizon.

I would give a month's pay for her thoughts, mused Ormsby to himself, as he stood watching the woman by his side. And then his fingers encircled her arm.

"Come, Lyda," he said. "Time to go to your cabin."

She smiled up at him, turned, and accompanied him without a word.

The six-day return trip to San Francisco was not nearly as relaxing as the trip to Hawaii. The Ormsbys took turns staying with Lyda, who was confined to her cabin, her meals being delivered by a steward.

Lyda was on her best behavior. She was tractable, charming, and quick with her low-throated laugh. The more time the Orsmbys spent with their charge, the more they were taken by her happy disposition, her wit, her engaging personality. As the trip wore on, Ormsby even agreed to bending the rules a bit and allowing her to eat dinner with them in the elegant ship's dining room. This served to make the grateful Lyda all the more cooperative.

The deputy sheriff had secretly hoped that during this time he and Nellie would be alone with her, they might be able to ingratiate themselves into Lyda's confidence. And, if they really hit the jackpot, wring a confession from her. But this was not in the cards.

It soon became apparent that Lyda Southard was not the confessing kind. She would respond to her captors' questions with those big, blue, bottomless eyes, and smile. "Why should I discuss things I didn't do?" was her stock answer.

As Ormsby became more and more aware of her attraction and sensual personality, he could understand why men had been trapped in the deadly web spun by this female black widow. He tried to form his own theory as to how this warm, gentle woman might kill so cold bloodedly — if indeed she had. As far as he could tell, the normal responses of kindliness and compassion were certainly included in Lyda's emotional inventory.

The normal human being, opined Ormsby, has feelings of love, caring, and responsibility for one's own actions, which keeps one from harming fellow human beings. So how could Lyda have killed with the same casualness one might show in swatting a fly? The burden of her crimes obviously did not weigh upon her mind. Therefore, she felt no necessity for confession.

And occasionally a disturbing thought would enter his mind. What if they had been wrong? What if Lyda was indeed innocent? It was true that the only evidence against the woman was circumstantial. Could she really have been a "typhoid carrier" as she claimed? Could it be that an unknown murderer with a diabolical plot was still lurking out there somewhere?

But then Ormsby would reconsider the evidence. The arsenic in the bodies that would have dispatched a regiment. The flypaper and pot found in the cellar of her former home. And maybe the most telling of all — the insurance policies. He had figured up the latest tally:

Ed Dooley, August 1915. Insurance: $2,000.
Bob Dooley, September 1915. Insurance: $2,500 and the farm.
Bill McHaffie, October 1918. No insurance, but the ranch.
Harlan Lewis, July 1919. Insurance: $10,000, plus the estate.
Ed Meyer, September 1920. Insurance: $12,000, not collected.

And Ormsby did not even like to speculate on the mysterious death of Lyda's three-year-old daughter in the fall of 1917.

All this, of course, was only what they knew. There were several gaps of many months in which the lady might have met and married other men whose ultimate destiny would never be known.

One evening Ormsby had watched his prisoner as she prepared to go to dinner. Arranging a feathered boa just right over her shoulders, she had hummed to herself as she dabbed a bit of perfume behind her ears. Then, finally groomed to her satisfaction, she calmly announced, "Shall we go to dinner?"

As she took Ormsby's arm, he thought to himself, I am escorting to dinner an innocent, gentle, attractive victim of extraordinary circumstances, or I am taking the arm of a clever, vicious, cold-blooded killer. These thoughts did little to whet Ormsby's appetite, but he felt confident that a dozen good men and true would make that decision in court.

Although Ormsby failed to wring a confession from his ward, the trip did have one very salubrious side effect: Nellie had met the woman whom she had accused of usurping the attentions of her husband. She quickly learned that Lyda was no mythical Lorelei bent on seducing her husband. In fact, the dreaded "other woman" was not to be dreaded at all. This woman whom Nellie had thought obsessed her husband was, in fact, quite plain. Especially when arising in the morning without her makeup, she looked downright dowdy. Lyda did, indeed, put her bloomers on one leg at a time just like any other woman.

Nellie would never be jealous of her husband's fixation on this woman again. For the temptress had turned out to be a tempest in a teapot.

In fact, Nellie, much to her surprise, was beginning to develop a genuine affection for her notorious roommate. And strangely enough, this warm feeling seemed to be shared by Lyda. One morning the two women were washing their stockings and undergarments in the bathroom lavatory of their stateroom when Nellie broached the subject of Lyda's background.

"Did you have a happy childhood, Lyda?" she asked.

Lyda drained the soapy water from the bowl and poured in rinse water. "Yes. I had a happy childhood. I loved my mother and father. They were just hardworking farm folks. And I grew up with lots of animals. I love animals. Don't you?"

"Yes. All except cats. I'm not too fond of cats."

"I love cats. They're so independent. So haughty and majestic. You never see a cat rolling in carrion like other animals do."

"I guess not."

"But I never cared for ranch life. I always thought there was more to life than rocking on the front porch and drinking warm lemonade or watching a magic lantern show. I love the bright lights. And dancing. And handsome men." She started swishing her laundry in the clean water and looked up at Nellie. "Don't you, Nellie?"

"Yes. I enjoy all those things. But instead of a handsome man, I settled for Virgil."

"I like Virgil. He's handsome in his own way."

"No. He's not handsome. But he's good on the inside. And he's my man. I love him very much."

"You're a lucky woman, Nellie."

"Yes." She took the wet laundry from Lyda and started squeezing the water out into the shower drain. "How about you, Lyda? You've had several husbands. Didn't you love them?"

An odd look came into Lyda's eyes. "Love? I'm not really sure what love is. I thought I was in love when I married my husbands. But after living with them for a while, my love seemed to die. Maybe it was puppy love. Or just infatuation. Or maybe I was too young to be married. I know that a lot of the allure of romance dies when you have to scrub dirty drawers and bib overalls. There's something about bib overalls that makes me want to throw up."

"I guess some people just aren't cut out to be a rancher's wife."

"I must be one of them." Lyda drained the rinse water, wiped her hands, and watched Nellie drape the laundry over the towel racks. "Come to think of it, maybe that's why I like Paul Southard better than any of my other husbands. He's not a farmer. And he looks so handsome in his navy uniform."

Their chores done, the two moved into the cabin, where the steward had placed a pot of tea and a tray of cookies on the nightstand. Lyda poured, handing a cup to Nellie. "I think I was born to this way of life," said Nellie, taking her cup.

"Me too." Lyda stirred sugar into her tea as she looked out of the porthole. "This," she said smiling, "is my cup of tea."

As they sipped their tea, Lyda suddenly put her hand out, taking Nellie's hand in her own. "Nellie, people have been saying awful things about me."

Nellie squeezed Lyda's hand. "Yes, Lyda. I know."

"They're not true, of course. No way could I ever do those terrible things they accuse me of."

Nellie's heart skipped a beat. Was she about to be privy to Lyda's innermost thoughts? "As I get to know you, Lyda, I find it hard to believe that you could be guilty of poisoning your husbands."

Lyda removed her hand from Nellie's. A shudder shot through her as she sat down on her bed. "It all is so horrible!" She lifted damp eyes to Nellie's. "I don't know how that arsenic could have ever gotten into the bodies of my husbands, but if someone put it there, I can only pray that they find the guilty party."

Nellie felt a surge of compassion as she reached out to the teary-eyed woman at her side. She put her arms around the sobbing woman. "There, there, Lyda. I know what you are going through. But you must look at the bright side. It is up to the state of Idaho to prove that you did those things. And as I understand it, there's not much hard evidence linking you to the crimes."

Lyda disengaged from her roommate, wiped her nose with her handkerchief. "There really isn't, is there?"

"No. And you will have a fair trial. Justice will be served. And as far as I know, there has never been a case of a woman going to the gallows."

"To the gallows!" Nellie bit her tongue, as this brought on a fresh torrent of tears.

"I meant to say," said Nellie, "that whoever perpetrated the crimes will have a fair hearing in Twin Falls. Idaho does not go overboard on capital punishment."

Lyda sniffed, poked at her eyes with her handkerchief. "Thank you, Nellie. For trying to cheer me up."

Nellie's heart went out to the small figure huddled on the bed. She patted her shoulder. "Try not to worry about it. Just enjoy the rest of the trip."

Lyda looked up at Nellie through red-rimmed eyes. She reached over and clutched her hand. "Thank you, Nellie. Thank you very much for being a friend."

"I'm happy to be your friend."

"I just hope they catch whoever did these terrible things."

"I'm sure they will."

Lyda stuffed her handkerchief into the sleeve of her dress, sniffed, and picked up her teacup. "Maybe I'll have just one more of those oatmeal cookies, Nellie. Would you pass them please?"

On June 7, the *Matsonia* steamed into San Francisco Harbor, to be met by an even larger crowd than had gathered to see Lyda Southard off in Honolulu. As the gangplank lowered, the press elbowed its way aboard, hoping to catch sight of the infamous murderess.

Once again, the famous movie star posing by the ship's rail was all but ignored as the press cameras focused on a rather plump woman dressed in a brown suit and a brown straw sailor hat. She was smiling and waving as she was escorted between a man and a woman toward the gangplank. Turning to her press agent, the jilted movie star snarled, "Who the hell *is* that woman?"

"Name's Lyda Southard," said the press agent.

"For God's sake, what does she do?"

"She murders husbands."

"Oh?" She smiled disarmingly at her aide. "Bully for her."

It was a nerve-wracking departure for Lyda to leave the quiet and seclusion of her ship's cabin and approach the throngs as she stepped slowly off the gangplank with head bowed at the entrance of Pier 32. Ukuleles on the lower deck were strumming the Hawaiian Tomi Tomi.

Brilliant camera flashes made the jostling crowd an even more eerie and frightening vista for Lyda, who hid behind dark-tinted glasses and a black fishnet veil. Reporters shot a steady succession of questions at her: "Did you poison your husbands?" "Is Southard going to join you?" "How was the food on the ship?"

"I shall have absolutely nothing to say until I reach Twin Falls," she mumbled repeatedly.

Ormsby and a squad of police officers, some mounted on horses, formed a phalanx that opened a path for Lyda to a waiting taxi. The crowd quickly closed in behind her. In the taxi, Ormsby suggested that before going to the luxury suite at the Hotel Whitcomb, they head for the jail to shake a convoy of Model T Fords that followed close behind them.

Lyda granted only one interview at the jail. Reporter Hazel Pedlar Faulkner of the *San Francisco Examiner* set the scene:

Dainty, friendly and refined, her slender hands folded in her lap, Lyda did not present the picture of a sinister murderer. Beside her on the jail cot were a half dozen leis and a well-worn fashion book. Lyda wore a tailored tan tricotine suit with a seal collar, a small brown sailor hat with a patterned veil, dark brown oxfords and silk hose. She turned a plain, narrow gold wedding ring around her finger as she spoke.

"I am not worried," she said. "Why should I be? I have a clear conscience. I have proof of the causes of death of all my husbands and little Laura Marie, my baby." Her lips trembled and tears welled in her eyes when she mentioned her daughter. The emotion quickly passed.

"I have been nervous because of my imprisonment and the unnecessary disgrace to my husband. I know as well as anything that I can clear myself. The evidence gathered against me is purely circumstantial. Their work is to prove the charges and that will not be easy because of the documents I hold.

"Life insurance was no object to me. I have had enough money. And what insurance my husbands carried were business propositions they took out without regard to me or without consulting me generally."

She spoke about her husband Southard, a chief petty officer with nine years experience in the navy. "I met him in San Pedro. I was lonesome and he was too, and we just took to each other from the start. The only fear that we had was that they might separate us somehow. That cannot be done legally."

When the last of the reporters left the Hall of Justice building, the Ormsbys emerged with their captive between them. At Lyda's request, they had removed her handcuffs. A small crowd quickly gathered around them. A few reporters climbed into their cars and followed the taxi containing Lyda and the Ormsbys. At the Hotel Whitcomb, the newsmen followed the trio into the lobby and crowded around the counter. A reporter looked over Ormsby's shoulder to see which rooms he had been assigned. He climbed the stairs as several other reporters followed.

A photographer stepped into the elevator with the Ormsbys and their charge. "I won't leave until Mrs. Southard personally refuses an interview." Ormbsy grabbed the reporter by the collar, pushed him out of the elevator, and sent him sprawling into the street.

As the deputy sheriff walked back into the hotel lobby dusting off his hands, the hotel manager was waiting with a large grin. Handing Ormsby a cigar, he said, "You can do that anytime you want, Sheriff."

On the third floor, Lyda was met by a small cluster of cameramen and reporters who were waiting at the elevator door. "Now let's be gentlemen and leave this lady alone," Ormsby said. The newsmen stepped back. When Ormsby opened the door, however, the reporter who had peered over his shoulder tried to sneak into the room. Ormsby grabbed him with both hands and pushed him against the far wall. "You better learn some manners, boy!" The reporter left, grumbling and looking back over his shoulder.

That Tuesday evening the Ormsbys took Lyda out on the town. They went to a dimly lit restaurant, finding to their relief that no one recognized them. That is, no one but an eager *San Francisco Chronicle* reporter, who tagged along unseen and wrote what he saw for the next day's paper.

The restaurant was filled with modishly gowned women and tuxedoed men. Gay music and chatter provided a festive atmosphere.

After dinner the threesome strolled through a downtown shopping district. Lyda smiled at the unknowing shop girls who waited on her. Obviously enjoying her anonymity as she strolled among the shoppers, Lyda reveled in the bright lights.

As a special treat, the Ormsbys took Lyda to the Orpheum Theater, where she watched a vaudeville show, "Singer's Midgets," starring Doris Duncan and "La Petite Cabaret." Lyda laughed heartily, not knowing her activities were being closely monitored by the shadowing reporter. She found out the next morning, however, when reporter Herb Westen by-lined the following article in the *San Francisco Call and Post*:

> With the grim specters of four dead husbands, a brother-in-law and her infant baby hovering near her, while the accusing finger of the law points at her and charges murder, Mrs. Lyda Eva Southard, psychological enigma, calmly spent yesterday seeing the sights of San Francisco.
>
> While two representatives of the law sat on either side, the reputed woman Bluebeard last night attended the Orpheum and laughed. The antics of the comedians tickled her risibilities, she applauded the dramatic and seemed to have about as much care in the world as an eighteen-year-old sub deb on a Sunday school picnic.
>
> The future? She smiles, a trifle shyly perhaps, but a bored light creeps around her eyes as if to her it is all a tedious legal jumble which will steal precious hours from her pursuit of happiness.

Wednesday morning Mrs. Ormsby and a cheerful Lyda came downstairs and ate breakfast in the hotel dining room. Then Ralph Wood, a friend of the Ormsbys, took the trio on a car trip around the city. They drove to Golden Gate State Park, shopped in China Town, and went to a motion picture in the early afternoon. Lyda seemed almost childlike and carefree as she laughed at the movie.

But when they returned to their hotel suite, Lyda's demeanor radically changed. Although the Ormsbys had endeavored to keep the papers away from Lyda for obvious reasons, she managed to get hold of a copy of the *San Francisco Call and Post*, which had been slipped under the door. She read the following report by Louise M. O'Hara, who had interviewed a criminologist who had examined Lyda's face and made conclusions with the logic of a palm reader:

"Her face is that of a weak woman," claimed the criminologist, "capable of committing the crimes of which she is accused, yet unconscious of her guilt.

"There is no stoicism in her character, but simply a great lack of understanding. A guilty woman would make a great show of righteous indignation, an innocent woman would be flat on her back from the ordeal, but Mrs. Southard simply does not realize she has committed a crime. She would be more concerned if she thought she would lose her supper tonight, than if told she was going to face the gallows. It's simply a case of her not realizing what she has done. She is utterly devoid of feeling.

"The short chin and the short upper lip, which slightly protrudes, and the peculiar construction of the nose just between the eyes are unmistakable signs of weakness, and those baby blue eyes show no distress as those of either a consciously guilty or an innocent woman would.

"If she committed the crimes of which she is accused, it was done as an animal would with simply a desire to get rid of something unpleasant with little regard for the means or the consequences."

Lyda's morale definitely took a nosedive after reading this account, and she confined herself to her bed, weeping quietly to herself.

Tired of being besieged by the press, and alarmed at what the oft-times vicious attacks of the press were doing to his charge, Ormsby declared a moratorium on further interviews. However, hoping to clear her name after the attack in the *San Francisco Call and Post*, Lyda wanted to grant one final interview before leaving San Francisco. Ormsby acquiesced, against his better judgment, and granted an interview request from a *San Francisco Bulletin* reporter. The news account quoted Lyda:

"I do not want to discuss the case, but I do want to tell how nice Mr. and Mrs. Ormsby have been to me. Everything has been perfectly lovely.

"I have not seen my mother since last September. I am anxious to be with her again even though our meeting will be tinged with sadness."

The Ormsbys rushed Lyda across the bay to an Oakland train that whisked them toward Idaho. Sheriff Sherman met the train at Wells, Nevada, where they disembarked and proceeded the remaining distance to Twin Falls by automobile.

The Twin Falls legal system lost no time in arraigning and formally charging Lyda Southard for the murder of Edward Meyer, and she was held without bail awaiting trial.

For the first time in months, Deputy Val Ormsby breathed a huge sigh of relief. Part of his mission had been accomplished. Now all he had to do was see his ward properly sentenced.

No sooner had Lyda been imprisoned than she was visited by her father. Sheriff Sherman ushered William Trueblood to the cell where Lyda waited. They rushed toward each other.

"Daddy."

Father and daughter wept as they embraced, rocking slowly back and forth in the dank jail cell.

Lyda's mood swings were upbeat after her arraignment on June 10. A reporter for the *San Francisco Examiner* captured her mood as she was quoted:

> The situation grows brighter with the hours. I see hope in the faces in the courtroom and in the faces of my friends I met in the corridors. I see hope in the faces of my lawyers and there is hope in the voice and eyes of dear old daddy.
>
> I cannot in these circumstances let this fight lag. They have dug up the pure little body of my dead baby; in the vile suspicion that I might have poisoned it. And I want that vindication that can only come at the end of a full hearing of all the facts. I want an immediate trial. We will disclose on how flimsy a basis they have hung these charges. I do not want to swelter all summer in the hot jail just because the state says it is not ready for trial.
>
> If the state is not ready then it should not have made public their charges against me. The hard part of all this is in the past now. My dread was in meeting the faces of the folks. What would there be in daddy's face?
>
> I knew his words would be kind — but the eyes. I dreaded to look into them. They are so truthful. If daddy had even a suspicion that I might be guilty, his eyes would tell it. All the way across on the long trip I have thought of those eyes and of daddy's evening prayers.
>
> As I knelt at my bed at night I have seen daddy's bowed head. And so I dreaded to meet him, yet yearned for him. Can't you see how jubilant I am? Daddy knows I am innocent. His eyes have told me so.

At Lyda's preliminary hearing, crowds of women thronged the courtroom. Judge O. P. Duvall ordered everyone out of the courtroom who didn't have seats, and had the doors locked. During a midafternoon recess the crowd in the lobby surged against the courtroom door and broke the glass. Oblivious to the judge's attempts to maintain order, Lyda nodded and waved to friends in the crowd.

This was all too much for Lyda's mother, who fainted and was carried to Sheriff Sherman's quarters on the fourth floor, where restoratives were applied. She later returned to sit in the gallery beside her husband, where she frequently burst into tears. On the second day of the preliminary hearing, Mrs. Trueblood did not appear.

For three months Lyda sat in her cell on the top floor of the Twin Falls courthouse, awaiting for the slow wheels of justice to grind. It was the same building in which she had applied for marriage licenses to wed three of the men she was now being accused of murdering: Robert Dooley, Billy McHaffie, and Edward Meyer.

Through the barred windows of her cell, Lyda could look out one side and see the high school campus. Here, not too many years ago, she had cheerfully welcomed the advances of young football players vying to see who could dip her long braids into their desk inkwell. Out of the other side of her cell she could see the city park where she had spent many summer evenings with both Meyer and McHaffie, listening to the band concerts.

As the date of the trial approached, Lyda's usually effervescent demeanor became more subdued, the twinkle in her eyes seemed to dim. This change was not lost on her attorneys, who became increasingly alarmed at some of her questions. She asked one of her lawyers, "Do you think they can convict me on circumstantial evidence?" And still later, when Dr. Wilson was called upon to minister to an infected finger, she asked him, "Doctor, can they really detect arsenic in a body that has been buried for several years?"

According to the *Portland Oregonian*, on the Sunday before the trial was to begin, Lyda prayed during services by Salvation Army Capt. J. F. Purdy. It was her first time since arriving in the jail.

In the prayer she asked forgiveness, saying that she had been unruly, not what her parents had hoped of her. She spent most of the night singing.

A few days later, before her trial was to begin, Lyda became hysterical during a religious service by Purdy. When she retired to her cell she began singing in a sweetly light mezzo-soprano voice the songs she had learned from Purdy.

The following day Purdy gave a sermon for Lyda and other jail inmates in the fourth floor jail. He talked about life beyond the grave, and Lyda, who had been sitting with a stoical expression on her face, burst into tears.

After the service Lyda seemed on the verge of confessing something to Purdy. Lyda asked him if she could trust him with a secret. She wanted to know if he would divulge in court what she would tell him.

"At this moment," said Purdy, "she appeared to be in great mental distress, and I believe she would have made me her confidant and probably would have provided me with all the details the prosecution seeks to possess, had I not declined to accept any confidences on condition that I would not reveal them if asked to by the prosecution."

Later Lyda denied making the statements to Purdy and said she would no longer talk to him.

Lyda's morale improved considerably when Paul Southard arrived on his furlough from the navy. Standing by the woman he loved, Southard adamantly refused to believe the charges that had been leveled against his wife. He was a loyal and faithful visitor to her cell at every opportunity, pledging his support, both moral and financial.

Chapter Twelve

On September 26, 1921, began what was to become the longest criminal trial to that time in history. Witnesses were brought in from all over the country, the press corps was represented by newshounds from major metropolitan papers. The notorious trial that had captured international attention had assumed an almost carnival atmosphere.

Farmers from nearby communities cranked up their Fords, Whippets, and Reos, or hitched up the buggy, packed up a lunch, stuffed in the wife and the kids, and sallied forth to partake of the grandest spectacle to ever hit Idaho. Gamblers were also attracted to the event, posting two to one odds that Lyda would go free. Betting was rampant. Every hotel in the area was crowded, the overflow having to take residence in towns as far away as Boise.

On opening day the courtroom was packed and stiflingly hot when Judge William Babcock banged his gavel and declared the proceedings had begun.

Four attorneys of the distinguished Twin Falls law firm of Guthrie and Mills represented the accused. The prosecution had also brought its big guns to bear, headed by the state's attorney general, Roy L. Black, County Attorney Frank L. Stephan, and lawyer E. A. Walters.

A hush fell over the hubbub as Lyda entered the courtroom on the arm of her husband. Dressed in a light summer frock, Lyda peered calmly around her, her eyes demurely somber. She smiled at the judge.

A week was spent in selecting a jury before the prosecution could plead its case. Peremptory challenges by both the prosecution and defense chewed up most of this time.

111

The jury panel was finally selected, and consisted of W. H. Cowhan, Twin Falls farmer; H. A. Crick, Kimberly carpenter; McCoy Hansen, Sturgeon farmer; Stacey Simpson, Kimberly farmer; George McPherson, Twin Falls farmer; F. L. Diffendorfer, Twin Falls stockman; S. R. Black, Twin Falls farmer; C. D. McKinley, Filer farmer; J. F. Denham, Kimberly bank teller; W. H. Spence, Kimberly farmer; E. S. True, Murtaugh farmer; and C. C. Silver, Twin Falls farmer. The average age of the jurors was about thirty-five.

Even with a plethora of witnesses, Prosecutor Stephan was not going to take any chances in this trial. He sent out an urgent request through the media for any information about a certain witness he wanted, even as the jury selection was winding down. He told reporters he was looking for a Buddy Thornberg, who came close to marrying Lyda a few months before Meyer met the widow.

Thornberg had been in Hoboken, New Jersey, ready to embark overseas to fight in World War I, when the armistice was signed. In early 1920, Thornberg came to Twin Falls and became a reporter for the *Daily News*. He met Lyda in the Grille Cafe, where she was a cashier using the name of Mrs. McHaffie even though she had been more recently married to Harlan Lewis. To quell rumors about her already mounting husband count, she had kept that to herself.

Lyda wooed Thornberg with incredibly feverish ardor. Thornberg often told his friends he was going to marry the rich widow from Montana. He told them that Lyda had a good business sense. She had advised him to keep his $10,000 government insurance policy, and take out a new policy from a private insurance company. But his friends pleaded with him not to marry Lyda, and he eventually broke off the romance and allegedly moved to Washington. He had not been heard from since.

Prosecutor Stephan naturally wanted that story to be told.

To simplify the case, Lyda had been charged only with the murder of Ed Meyer, but evidence pointing to the killing of other men was admitted. The prosecution fired its opening broadside, presenting Virgil Ormsby as the first in a long parade of witnesses. Their testimony laid the strategic battle plan for what was to become a blistering attack on the campaign of Lyda Southard's defense lawyers.

Ormsby was on the stand for several days, detailing the results of his long, torturous investigation. Chemists and laboratory experts testified about the poison that had been found in the bodies of the men that the state charged Lyda had killed. It was important to counter the defense's strategy of introducing doubt into the minds of the jurors about the source of Meyer's poisoning.

John W. Gilbaugh, chemist from a Portland chemical company, testified that Royal Balmo, the embalming fluid used on Harlan Lewis's corpse, did not contain arsenic. Charles P. Hendricks of the Embalmer's Supply Company, the Seattle manufacturer of the fluid used to embalm Edward Meyer, also testified that his company's fluid contained no arsenic.

Defense Attorney Mills tried to shoot holes in the prosecution's case by contending that Lyda's many husbands could have been poisoned by arsenic in some way other than by mouth. He grilled Herman Harms, state chemist for Utah, for nearly two hours, the confrontation electrifying the courtroom:

"First degree murder is a very serious charge, is it not, Mr. Harms?" asked Mills.

"Yes, of course," responded Harms.

"So we're agreed," said Mills, rising from his chair. "You do understand that the punishment for such a crime could be death by hanging. By hanging, Mr. Harms!"

"Yes."

"Then we want to be absolutely sure what we say about the death of Mr. Meyer, don't we?"

"Absolutely."

Mills walked to the bench slowly, and then pointed a finger at Harms. "Have you been paid for your testimony today, Mr. Harms?"

"Yes, I have." Harms fiddled with his necktie.

"How much?"

"One hundred and twenty-five dollars each for the four bodies I examined."

"Uh huh. Do you also receive money for your services in court?"

"Yes. Twenty-five dollars per day." There was an audible gasp from people in the courtroom. "But this is a much smaller sum than is usually paid for expert services of this nature."

Mills shook his head condescendingly. "Now consider." He paused for effect. "Would it not be possible for a body to take up arsenic from the soil?"

"Such a possibility would be very remote indeed."

"Well, Mr. Harms, would it not be possible for arsenic to seep from one body containing it into another after death?"

"No. It would not."

"Couldn't arsenic gain access to buried bodies by seeping through the soil from orchards nearby . . . where it has been used for spraying?"

"This would be a very unlikely contingency."

Mills chuckled to himself, seemingly finding something amusing in Harms's response. "Did you ever hear of the body taking up arsenic from the clothing . . . the coffin . . .the box in which it was buried?"

"I have heard of it," replied Harms, "in certain low-lying countries where bright colored clothes are worn at burial. Arsenic dyes used in the manufacture of such clothes might result in small quantities of the poison working into the body."

"Did you ever hear of arsenic poisoning by vapor or fumes?"

"Yes. Animals have been poisoned by smelter smoke around Salt Lake."

"Did you ever hear of arsenic poisoning through the use of intoxicating liquors?"

"I have never heard of an instance of this."

On a notebook on the prosecution's table, Prosecutor Stephan scrawled the word "Absurd."

The defense attorney leaned in. "Did you ever hear of trees, plants, and vegetables containing arsenic poison?"

"Faint traces of arsenic have been found in certain plants and vegetables, but the presence of a drug in this way is in no sense injurious."

"Thank you, Mr. Harms." Mills turned to the judge. "That is all the questions I have for this witness, your honor."

Stephan rose quickly to redirect. "Did you not earlier tell us that the organ specimens from Mr. Meyer's body contained lethal amounts of arsenic, Mr. Harms?"

"Yes," replied the witness. "That was my testimony."

"What are the chances that the lethal dose could have come from the soil at the cemetery, from his burial clothes, from other corpses in the cemetery, or from embalming fluid?"

"So small that I would conclude it is virtually impossible."

"And why is that?" Stephan asked.

"Because the arsenic was found in like amounts in every organ I examined, and even in hair and fingernails. That kind of distribution only happens in a live body with blood circulating the poison."

Stephan's eyes focused on the jury as he said, "No further questions."

As the trial wore on, the astute prosecuting attorney noticed that the lengthy testimony by experts using almost indecipherable technical jargon was beginning to have a stultifying effect on the court attendance. After observing a couple of the jurors nodding off, Stephan decided to jar the assemblage awake. He called a well-to-do widow, Mrs. Fred James, to the witness stand.

Dressed in the latest finery, including a plumed-feather hat resembling a molting partridge, this handsome woman created an audible stir in the courtroom. Through this witness the prosecution skillfully relayed to the jury and the spectators a glimpse of the highfaluting circles Lyda was moving in, even as her husband lay writhing in pain on his deathbed at the Blue Lakes Ranch. Mrs. James had been staying at the plush Rogerson Hotel while Lyda lived there. The jurors were told that this elegant hostelry — Twin Falls' finest — sported a carriage taxi service with a Negro driver for its patrons, and a pianist and a violinist serenaded its diners in its posh dining room.

Mrs. James testified as to her surprise that the newlywed wife of a farm worker would want to stay at the hotel away from her husband. Or could even afford to.

Attorney Stephan was pleased to see the jurors were now awake. "At the time that her husband was sick in the hospital, did Lyda Meyer tell you she was planning to leave the area?"

"I must tell you, while I was at the hotel I knew Mrs. Meyer as Mrs. McHaffie, and did not know she was married to Mr. Meyer at first."

"Did she try to keep it a secret, Mrs. James?"

"Not really. She just never mentioned it. She talked a lot about going to Butte, Montana."

"To Butte, Montana?"

"Yes, sir. She said she owned wheat fields there, and she had to go and take care of things because the elevators had shut down."

"I see. Go on, Mrs. James."

"Then one night she came in looking kind of . . .you know . . . distraught. It was then she told me she was married to Mr. Meyer and had been out to the ranch to see him. She said she had been married three weeks and hardly anyone knew about it. And now her husband was ailing."

"What did she tell you about her husband's sickness?"

"She told me her husband had ptomaine poisoning and had been brought to the county hospital. After that she made frequent trips to the hospital."

"Did she ever tell you how her husband was doing?"

"Once she remarked he was somewhat better and could take some broth. But a short time later she said he couldn't get well."

"Did you see Mrs. Meyer on the day her husband died?" Stephan asked.

"I saw her fifteen minutes after her husband died."

Stephan could feel the energy in the courtroom. "And where was this, Mrs. James?"

"In her hotel room. I went into her room and found her packing her things. She seemed quite upset."

"What did she say?"

Mrs. James took a deep breath, dredging her memory. "She said Ed Meyer had passed on. Then she sort of ranted, saying, 'Oh, well. He only married me for my money anyway. There's been a lot of talk going around that I poisoned him, and they're going to hold a postmortem.'" The witness stopped for a moment, dramatically dabbing at the corner of her eye with her handkerchief.

"Please continue, Mrs. James."

"Well, sir, I naturally tried to cheer her up. I said they often do those things in a case of sudden death."

"Did you ask her why she was packed?"

"Yes. Yes, I did."

"And what did she say?"

"Well, sir, she almost had a tizzy fit. 'They'll not find me,' she said. 'I'm going to beat it to Los Angles or San Francisco.'"

"Is that the last you saw of Lyda Meyer?"

"Not quite. We had dinner later at the hotel dining room. While we were eating, some of the nurses from the hospital came in. Lyda jumped up from the table and left, saying, 'I'm leaving. I don't want those nurses watching me.'"

"Did you see her on the day of her husband's funeral?"

"Yes. That was the last time I saw her. When she returned home from the funeral, I saw her walk into the hotel. She took off her mourning hat as she walked in, and placed it under her arm. She went right up to her room and immediately changed into her street clothes."

Stephan nodded, turned a firm face to the jury. "Your witness, Mr. Mills."

In spite of the overwhelming evidence, the oddsmakers still favored Lyda to be acquitted. Although most of them considered her guilty, the past history of Twin Falls County jurisprudence had tipped the scales of justice in Lyda's favor. Of the nine people who had been tried for murder in the county since its incorporation, only two had been convicted.

Weeks passed, the inexorable legal machinery clanking on. The bright fires in Lyda's eyes seemed to have been banked by the grinding progress of the trial. She sat stoically, day after day, apparently oblivious to the glass jars now surrounding her that had been introduced as evidence by the prosecution to substantiate the arsenic content of Lyda's victims.

In spite of being in the company of the pickled parts of her dead spouses' organs, Lyda would smile at the jury and solemnly bow to the press as she entered the courtroom to take her seat. One morning she said to Sheriff Sherman's wife, her matron, "Fix my hair nicely today, Mother Sherman. I want to make a good impression."

But as the trial wore on, it became obvious that Lyda was going to have to make more than just a good impression. As other evidence began to accumulate, it became apparent that the accused might have become a bit careless with her arsenic.

One witness tried to connect Lyda with the disappearance of a Ben Cheesman, an Idaho auto salesman, who was alleged to have met Lyda after the death of husband number three, Harlan Lewis. He was supposed to have taken her to the Pacific Northwest with him. Cheesman mysteriously dropped from sight, leaving his trunk in a hotel room and never calling for $600 in salary that was due him. This testimony was thrown out of court, ruled hearsay evidence, but it was not lost on the jurors who were hanging on every word.

As one by one the witnesses were called to the stand to be examined and cross-examined, several in particular stood out as presenting particularly damaging testimony. One of these was B. V. Squires, bunkmate of Ed Meyer before he was married, who told of the evening meal at the ranch boarding house, when he had dined with the newlyweds and some of the ranchhands.

"Directly after supper I went out fishing for half an hour," testified Squires. "I began to get sick to my stomach and then I had an attack of cramps. Returning to the tent where Ed and I bunked together, I went to bed and the pains kept me awake all night. About nine o'clock Ed came in, groaning, and knelt down at the side of my bed, with his hands on his stomach. As I lay there, I asked him what the matter was, but he just continued to groan. Then he left without speaking. The next morning I felt so bad I only worked half a day."

"What did you have to eat that night?" asked prosecutor Frank Stephan.

"A few beans, bread and butter, and a cup of coffee."

"When did you next talk to the defendant?"

Squires blew his nose. "Sunday. The day Ed was taken to the hospital. Lyda came to my tent for turpentine. She said, 'The doctor said he can't live long. We're going to work on him and see what we can do.'"

Nor was Lyda's defense enhanced when Mrs. Carrie Howe, cook at the Blue Lakes Ranch, was put on the stand. After being sworn in, she was interrogated by prosecutor Frank Stephan. "When did you know that the defendant and Ed Meyer were married?" asked the prosecutor.

"Late in August Ed came back to the ranch and said they were married," Mrs. Howe replied.

"Did Mrs. Southard return to the ranch after her marriage?"

"She did not."

"Do you know where she stayed?"

"She was staying at the Rogerson Hotel in town. Lyda said her doctor told her that she had symptoms of typhoid fever and that it was best for her to stay in town. She was paying forty dollars a month for her room and decided to keep it. She said there was no place to put her clothes at the ranch."

The subject of poison flypaper was then brought up by the prosecution. Questioned as to whether the defendant brought anything to the ranch, Mrs. Howe replied: "Lyda had some flypaper, which she moistened and placed in dishes on the kitchen table the same day she arrived. It was left standing a couple of days, and I threw it out. After Ed's death I found two packages of unused flypaper in a dresser drawer in the room they used while at the ranch."

The poison flypaper was introduced as evidence, then the prosecution, indicating the packages, asked, "Have you seen these before?"

"Yes, sir," Mrs. Howe responded, nodding her head.

"Who took care of Ed Meyer during his sickness at the ranch?"

"Lyda did."

"Did the defendant tell you what she was worth?"

"Lyda said to me once that she would come into the estate of a former husband in Montana on October first. It was supposed to amount to about sixty thousand dollars."

"While Meyer was sick, did you ever discuss him with the defendant?"

"Some, " Mrs. Howe replied. "She told me she didn't love him like she should love a man she was married to. I spoke up and said Ed was a good man and should be treated right. Lyda said she'd do that, but it was going to be hard to settle down. I saw her just after her husband died. She called me to her car and said, 'Ed's just passed away. You probably heard stories going around about his death. If anything happens, I want you to be a witness for me.' I told her that if the remarks were true she ought to be punished for it."

Martha M. Garrett, general nurse at the county hospital, was called to the stand by the prosecution. She stated she had seen Lyda Meyer give her husband a glass of water on several occasions, and had fed him tea and toast.

"Did you have any conversation with Mrs. Meyer?" asked the prosecuting attorney.

"Yes. On one visit to the hospital she said, 'I know he's not going to get any better. I see death in his face.'"

Sidney B. All, Twin Falls druggist, stated in his testimony that Mrs. Meyer had come into the store some time after August 13 and had asked for poisonous flypaper.

"How much did you sell her?" asked prosecutor Stephan.

"Either fifty cents' or a dollar's worth. An uncommon amount. It sold for a nickel a package. I asked her what she was going to do with all that flypaper. 'I'm going to take it to the ranch,' she said. 'Flies are a big problem.'"

Harriet W. Roberts, Dr. Coughlin's secretary, testified that when Mrs. Meyer first called the doctor's office to report her husband's sickness, she repeatedly downplayed the urgency of her husband's condition.

"'There's no hurry, anytime will do,'" Roberts said Mrs. Meyer had told her.

Adding to the growing pile of evidence that was accumulating was the testimony of Dr. Edward F. Rhodenbaugh, Idaho state chemist. The pickled organs carved from the corpse of Ed Meyer that had been introduced into evidenced were now referred to during the doctor's testimony. They were identified as samples from Meyer's kidney, liver, spleen, and small and large intestines. The prosecution asked Dr. Rhodenbaugh, "How much is a lethal dose of arsenic?"

"From half a grain up," answered the doctor.

"How much do you estimate the organs of the samples you examined contained?"

"Two-thirds of a gram."

"Is it not true," asked Stephan, boring in, "that when arsenic is taken into the system it is disseminated throughout the body?"

"Yes," answered Rhodenbaugh. "It can be found in all the organs of the body. The bones, hair . . . even the fingernails."

"If this were true, how much arsenic would you estimate there was in Meyer's body?"

"Judging the weight of an average man's body to be about 75 kilograms, or 165 pounds, his body would have contained 9.8 grains of arsenic."

"And what did you say would be a killing dose?"

"About half a grain."

Stephan did some quick calculations. "Then in your opinion, Doctor, Mr. Meyer had absorbed enough arsenic to kill about twenty men."

"Perhaps. At least five men."

"No other questions."

Inadvertently relieving the tenseness of the trial was the testimony of P. J. Grossman, Twin Falls County coroner, when asked of the care he had taken of Ed Meyer's body while it was lying on the marble slab in the morgue.

"What do you use that embalming lotion for?" asked Homer C. Mills, counsel for the defense.

"Oh, we rub it on the dead man's face with a sponge."

"Is that all you use it for?"

"The hands of the corpse are massaged with it, too."

After a pause, Mills pressed the witness. "Are you sure that's all?"

"Well, " drawled the coroner, "some folks use it for shaving lotion."

There was much tedious examination regarding the medical results of the autopsy. The defense had built its case mainly on the introduction of the death certificate, which had been signed by the doctor as being the result of typhoid. The prosecution was quick to leap on this as a mistake by the attending physician, and produced many medical witnesses to testify to the fact.

A bitter clash between the defense and the prosecution ensued during the final days of the trial. The last-ditch attempts by the defense to have the case thrown out of court for lack of evidence were buried under the mountain of circumstantial evidence that had built up.

In the final days of the trial, Lyda took the stand, looking neat and prim with the help of her matron. Although she smiled beguilingly at the jury, her testimony under examination and cross-examination seemed to have little effect on the jurors. Her testimony consisted simply of a sweeping denial of everything. She reiterated the fact that she was obviously a "typhoid carrier," which explained the deaths of her husbands—as attested to by their death certificates. She admitted she had an almost fanatic aversion to flies, which explained the flypaper. And as for the insurance taken out on her husbands, that was merely the procedure practiced by most newlyweds who truly loved one another.

Finally the long trial ground to its closing. The attorneys for both sides summed up, Judge Babcock charged the jury, and the jurors filed out. It was 4:45 p.m. on Wednesday afternoon, November third. All that remained was the verdict of the jury.

An almost audible sigh of relief issued from the Twin Falls townsfolk as the decision of the long trial was finally put into the hands of the panel. The three-ring circus had shattered the normal routines of the city for nearly six weeks. Sewing circles and afternoon card parties had been postponed by the women; men's pool halls and poker parlors drew more dust than devotees. Now, with almost unbearable tension, the populace awaited the decision of one of America's most famous murder trials.

The following afternoon the jury returned from its cloister. As they filed in and took their seats, the jury foreman handed a slip of paper to Judge

Babcock. He took one look at it and, expressionless, handed the slip to the court clerk.

A hush came over the packed courtroom, scored only by the swishing sound of fans in the hands of the female attendees. In stentorian tones the county clerk read from the slip of paper in his hand.

"We find the defendant guilty of murder in the second degree as charged in the information."

After a brief second of shocked silence, the courtroom erupted into a wild frenzy. One woman fainted, many clapped, and the hubbub of bettors claiming their winnings drowned out the judge's gavel banging for order.

Lyda sat stiffly in her chair, oblivious to the pandemonium about her. Then an almost imperceptible smile toyed with her lips. Perhaps she was relieved at escaping the gallows. In truth, the verdict was contrary to Idaho state law, which specifically stated: "All murder which is precipitated by means of poison . . . is murder in the first degree." The jurors, obviously having no stomach for seeing a woman hang, had concurred on the lesser charge. Now, adding yet another twist to this bizarre trial, the judge had to cope with an illegal finding by the jury. What would be the consequences of this infraction?

On a far side of the courtroom, completely unnoticed, sat a medium-sized man with a large nose and closely set, steady eyes. A half-smile also played with the lips of Virgil H. Ormsby, Twin Falls deputy sheriff, as he rocked back in his chair, arms folded, and stared with glowing eyes at the woman he, more than anyone else, had been responsible for bringing to justice. For a brief moment, his eyes met Lyda's. His half-smile turned into a broad grin. She tore her eyes away and addressed herself to the photographers swarming around her.

After the verdict, Lyda seemed to be in a much happier mood — almost as if a huge burden had been lifted from her shoulders. She told her cell mate, in jail for theft, that she was relieved.

Sheriff Sherman searched her cell for suicide devices, because she had repeatedly stated throughout the trial that she would never serve a day in prison; that she would kill herself first. She playfully helped Sherman in his search.

Then she diligently mopped the floor as she hummed popular tunes. In response to a query from a reporter on the *Boise Capital News*, she said, "They are talking about an appeal. But I don't know."

The following Monday, Judge Babcock delivered his sentence. Lyda Southard was sentenced to serve from ten years to life in the state penitentiary at Boise. It was recommended by the judge and the prosecuting attorneys that the maximum sentence be carried out.

Lyda was taken to Boise by Sheriff Sherman, processed by the prison officials, and assigned a cell. The doors of the women's prison clanged shut behind her.

Only then did it sink into the muddled mind of her husband, Paul Vincent Southard, that it would be difficult to pursue a life of connubial bliss with one's mate behind the gray walls of the forbidding Idaho state prison.

The hapless husband filed for divorce.

Thus it appeared that the saga of one of the country's most enigmatic women, the celebrated marrying murderess, would end behind the spartan, sandstone walls of the women's section of the Idaho State Penitentiary; that this woman, who could allegedly kill in cold blood, yet charm the pants off a prospective husband, was doomed to spend the rest of her life behind iron bars where she would be soon forgotten by all save a handful of grieving relatives of the deceased.

But anyone who thought this incarceration would close the book on a mild-mannered, pretty spouse-slayer did not know Mrs. Lyda Trueblood-Dooley-McHaffie-Lewis-Meyer-Southard.

Chapter Thirteen

The Idaho penitentiary is a menacing, stark cluster of buildings on the outskirts of Boise, Idaho. The cornerstone of this gloomy complex was laid on the Fourth of July, 1870, with much ceremonial hoopla and fireworks.

The *Idaho Tri-Weekly Statesman*, Idaho's leading newspaper at the time, made the comment: "A general attendance of every age and sex is requested to view an edifice that may someday be their home — and not even the wisest knows how soon." In 1872 the first prisoners were admitted.

Now, half a century later, Idaho's famed Lady Bluebeard took up residence there, becoming the prison's most notorious inmate. The penitentiary rested at the bottom of a hill called Tablerock, from which hardened prisoners had mined the sandstone that would build the new house of correction. Buildings of the men's quarters were surrounded by gray walls fourteen feet high; the women prisoners, few in number, were housed in a high-fenced enclosure across the street from the men's prison.

The vehicle carrying Lyda Southard and Sheriff Sherman stopped before the prison office. Sherman rang a bell to summon the turnkey, and the door swung open. No word was spoken. They stepped inside, the door clanged shut behind them; a great key was turned in the lock, and iron bars and stone walls would now protect society from the likes of Lyda Southard.

She was taken to the front office to be Bertilloned — prison parlance for being mugged, weighed, measured, fingerprinted, and all scars and marks noted. She was then taken to the bathhouse by the prison matron, given a bath, and assigned number 3052, indicating she was the three-thousand and fifty-second prisoner to be received in the Idaho State Penitentiary. She was then delivered to her cell.

The women's quarters were small, claustrophobic cubicles surrounding an open area in which the prisoners could mingle until lockup time in the evening, when they had to return to their cells. A grassy, weedy area separated the blockhouse from the towering sandstone walls that surrounded it.

The penitentiary had housed such male luminaries as Diamondfield Jack Davis, an alleged gunslinger and mining entrepreneur; a member of the Dalton "Hole In the Wall" gang; and the famous Harry Orchard, who assassinated Idaho's ex-governor. Aside from Lyda, however, there were very few celebrities in the women's ward.

Lyda found her prison mates included a female bootlegger who had also induced a girl to enter a house of prostitution; a woman convicted of rape, who had allowed a man to live with her thirteen year-old daughter; and a woman given four years for stealing a ham. According to the prosecutor who put the pork purloiner away, his winning argument was, "The ham was a young ham, it was not strong, it was shown at the trial that the ham could not have traveled of its own volition."

This was rivaled in imagination only by the inmate in the men's prison who swore he was imprisoned for stealing a rope. "How was I to know," he pleaded in self-defense, "that when I got the rope home there was a horse tied to the end of it?"

Lyda saw inmates come and go; old-timers completing their sentence, new ones arriving. Although not the class of people Lyda liked to associate with, they were receptive to her charms, and she was pleasant but close-lipped about her own past. Her advice to the other women prisoners was succinct: "Don't talk and you'll have less to regret."

Although time might have dragged for Lyda during her years of imprisonment, events on the outside proceeded at a fast clip. Presidents Calvin Coolidge and Herbert Hoover were sworn into office during those years. A young, handsome flyer named Charles Augustus Lindbergh made a stop in Boise; Knute Rockne's Notre Dame team won nine out of nine football games; the Charleston became the dancing rage; Amelia Earhart became the first woman to fly across the Atlantic; and not to be outdone, a lass named Lizzie Borden became a central figure in a Fall River, Massachusetts, murder mystery by allegedly chopping up her father and stepmother with an axe.

The pages of the calendar slowly flipped by. Being an accomplished seamstress, Lyda sewed her own dresses; unlike the men, the women were not required to wear uniforms. She would spend the long, cold winter months sewing, reading, and playing the Victrola in her cell. Although Lyda prided herself on her record collection, it was the stirring strains of "When the Saints Go Marching In" that most often wafted out on the crisp winter air.

The women did their own cooking in a common kitchen, eating at a long table set up in the center of the building. A communal shower served hygenic needs, slopjars under the bunks handled nocturnal needs.

Lyda eagerly looked forward to the summer months, as these gave her the opportunity to work off the fat that had accumulated during winter's hibernation. The inactivity caused her to look wide-hipped and dumpy, a condition of great concern to the vain woman who had always prided herself on her appearance. When spring came, faint aromas from fruit trees in the valley wafted over the walls, stirring Lyda's blood. She loved flowers and had always had gardens in her homes in the outside world.

She asked permission from Warden Wheeler to plant a garden on the inside of the prison wall. Certainly seeing no harm in that, he gave her permission. Lyda worked hard, planting flowers and grass provided by the prison authorities. She delighted in tending her flora, particularly enchanted by the new vines that crept up the drab prison walls as if making their bid for freedom.

As the years crawled by, Lyda became more and more a trustworthy member of the institution. Relaxation of some of the prison regulations accompanied this trust. She was even allowed to visit with some of the male trusties. Although her face was becoming a lined roost for crow's feet, and her figure was more portly than petite, she still possessed some inner sensuality that men found intriguing. She was one of the most popular inmates in the prison, cheerfully holding court for the many reporters and photographers who never seemed to satiate their reader's interest in Idaho's most famous woman.

Deputy Sheriff Virgil Ormsby was an infrequent visitor, entering the grim gate of the women's prison to chat with the woman who had consumed such a large slice of his life. She was always cordial, friendly, and dressed up in her newest frock as she received him, laughing and smiling as if she were inviting him in for high tea.

Oddly, Ormsby's wife, Nellie, was an even more frequent caller to the shut-in. Ever since playing the role of custodian on the ship that had brought Lyda from Honolulu, Nellie had developed a genuine liking for the woman of intrigue.

Nellie was not at all sure Lyda was guilty, a fact she had expressed on many occasions to her very skeptical husband. "It is inconceivable," maintained Nellie, "that that kind, warm woman could possibly be guilty of such heinous crimes." When her husband pointed out the stacks of overwhelming circumstantial evidence and the decision of the jury as to her guilt, Nellie would just sigh and say, "Well, if that is the case, Lyda must be one of those multiple personalities the psychiatrists are talking about. Maybe something goes off in her head that changes her into another person.

A madwoman who commits those horrible crimes. But the Lyda I know is a very sweet and loving person. I feel very, very sorry for her."

And the feeling of friendship was mutual, as Lyda very much looked forward to Nellie's visits. The two would visit for hours in the courtyard of the women's ward, snacking on the cookies and pastries Nellie would bring in her picnic basket.

Another of Lyda's frequent visitors was a trusty named Harry Orchard, the most notorious inmate of the men's prison. Orchard had been involved in a labor union scandal that eventually led to the famous assassination of Idaho's ex-governor, Frank Steunenberg. By the simple expedient of planting a bomb that detonated when the governor opened the gate to his front yard, Orchard had effectively eliminated his adversary.

This case had also made national news, and eventually embraced the talents of several young lawyers named Jack Hawley, William E. Borah, and Clarence Darrow. After a stormy session of trials and recriminations, Orchard was sent to the Idaho State Penitentiary to be hung in the prison gallows. His sentence was later commuted to life imprisonment in the penitentiary.

It was only logical that Lyda and Harry Orchard would gravitate to one another, spending considerable time together discussing their mutual horticulture interest.

Although a subject seldom mentioned beyond the prison walls, sex occasionally took place behind them. Some of Lyda's prison mates were known to have performed provocative stripteases for the benefit of the tower guards. A few trusties also proved less than trusting as they used their privilege to be sure the women's ward was properly serviced at all times.

Lyda had little to do with most of the trusties, whom she considered to be much below her social status. But she was, on occasion, observed by local townspeople in the company of the warden himself, discretely picnicking on the shores of nearby Lake Lowell. Lyda was not one to let her beguiling sexuality rust.

It was eight years after Lyda's incarceration that Deputy Sheriff Virgil Ormsby suffered a paralytic stroke near his home in Twin Falls. He was immediately hospitalized and given the best medical attention Twin Falls had to offer. Slowly Ormsby fought his way to recovery, and he was almost conducting his duties in a normal manner when he was hit by a second stroke on December 29, 1929. This time he did not regain consciousness as he was carried to his home in Twin Falls. He died hours later in Nellie's arms. The coroner listed the cause of death as cerebral hemorrhage apoplexy.

The December 30, 1929, edition of the *Twin Falls Times* carried Virgil

H. Ormsby's obituary on the front page. The headline read "Pioneer Twin Falls Citizen Called To Rest." The long years of sleuthing, pursuing, and being the man most responsible for the apprehending of one of the nation's most heinous murderers was encapsulated in the *Times* into one paragraph of his obituary, which read:

"He had successful administrations as juvenile officer and deputy sheriff. It was during one of his terms as deputy sheriff that the Lyda Southard case was tried, and he was assigned to return Mrs. Southard from Honolulu."

And thus, Deputy Sheriff Virgil H. Ormsby was laid to rest. Lyda Southard sent flowers to the funeral.

But the saga of Lady Bluebeard was not to be concluded by the death of her nemesis.

The year following Virgil Ormsby's death was Lyda's ninth spring in captivity. From her cell, she could hear the voices of the men trusties working on the road outside. The men were building a new home for the trusties only a few yards from the wall of the women's prison, and Lyda enjoyed the sounds of the male voices permeating the dank confines of her cell block.

On a particularly warm day, she walked across the prison yard to the iron door with the curved top that fronted the road where the men were working. There was a small peephole in the old rusty door. Lyda put one eye against the hole and silently watched the trusties going about their business. Her blue eye fixed on the figure of one particular worker as he moved back and forth with his hammer in hand. An unprepossessing-looking man at best, the trusty wore thick glasses, slouched as he walked, and was of small build. But there was an easy grace about the man, and the masterful way in which he handled his tools seemed to have an effect on Lyda.

Perhaps the power of her scrutiny made the trusty conscious of her observation. At any rate, he found an excuse to go near the iron door, and keeping a wary eye on the guards, he planted an eye on the peephole. He was startled to see the large blue eye blinking at him from the other side. His muttered apologies were swept aside as Lyda whispered to him in a low voice. A short exchange resulted, then the trusty went about his business.

The summer passed, the new building for the trusties was completed. Being so close to the women's prison, its barred second-story windows on one side looked down into the women's enclosure. The particular trusty who had communicated with Lyda at her door spent a lot of time at one of these windows, gazing toward the women's courtyard. When Lyda appeared in the yard and gave a sign that she had recognized him, his face would light up like a guardhouse searchlight. It seemed out of character that Lyda would cotton to this man, as his thick, beer-bottle-bottom eyeglasses did little to enhance his personal appearance. Yet Lyda seemed to respond to his schoolboy advances.

When the next spring rolled around, Lyda planted more flowers. But her climbing roses needed a support to help them reach the top of the wall. She asked the warden if she could have some heavy trellises made. The warden, being on such good terms with his favorite prisoner, quickly granted permission. Oddly enough, it was the nearsighted trusty who constructed the iron trellises, brought them to the women's enclosure, and placed them where the rose tendrils could get a foothold. The roses quickly took to the trellises, climbing upward toward the sky. Lyda seemed to take immense pride in her flowering achievements.

The spring of 1931 came early, along with a couple of changes that influenced Lyda's tenure in captivity. Her clandestine inamorato — the nearsighted trusty — was paroled, which seemed to create a small void in Lyda's life. Secondly, a change in the political climate saw the replacement of Lyda's friendly warden with a stern-faced disciplinarian named E. R. Thomas.

The new warden took out his new broom and started to sweep the prison clean. He made many changes, tightened the screws on security, and worked hard at making the Idaho State Penitentiary a model prison. Among other things, a prison inspection revealed the rusty iron door with the peep-hole in it. Checking it out, the warden was surprised to see a blue eye at the aperture gazing unblinkingly at the outside world. A half hour later he returned, took another look at the door. He was startled to find the eye was still there.

When Warden Thomas found out the eye belonged to Lyda Southard, he promptly had the iron door covered with a new heavy wooden door. The new custodian was taking no chances. He wondered about the woman, determined he would have her watched carefully.

It was the night of May 4, 1931. A small rock bounced off the roof of the women's prison house. Shortly after, a Victrola in one of the cells began to play. The lively strains of "When the Saints Go Marching In" came spilling out into the night air. Then an apparition seemed to eerily emerge from the stone side of the building.

The figure pressed tightly against the building's stone wall, hugging the shadows. The phantom wore trousers. It moved purposefully, heading for the prison wall. Reaching the rosebeds, it stopped, listening. There was no unusual movement in the guard towers. Then there was a grunt as one of the trellises was laboriously removed from the ground. It was stripped of its clinging rose vines and stood on end. A second trellis was removed from the flowerbed. Its top end fitted precisely into the bottom end of the other trellis. The two were connected. The sturdy iron ladder was then raised to touch the top of the wall.

The figure crouched down, picked up a coiled rope made of shredded bedclothes, looped it over its shoulder. The wraith remained motionless, blending into the shadows. And then silver clouds scudded across the moon, and for a brief time the prison was in shadow. Quickly taking advantage, the figure picked up the loose end of a garden hose that was firmly attached to a workbench, scaled the ladder, reached the top of the wall, uncoiled the rope of bedclothes, tied one end to the end of the garden hose that barely reached the top, then tossed the other end over the wall. In a flash the escapee slid down the rope, paused for a moment on the ground, then took off at top speed into the night.

Across the road, a guard with a submachine gun came out of the sentry's tower to patrol the wall of the men's enclosure. The swinging searchlight showed nothing amiss, the guard continued his rounds. The moon came out from behind the clouds, illumining a prison that seemed to be settling down for the night.

Panting heavily from the exertion of racing across the stubble field, the figure jumped into the front seat of the Hupmobile roadster parked in a copse of trees near the prison. The man behind the wheel started the engine, put the car in gear, and started backfiring down the road. The driver turned toward the figure seated beside him, squinting through the thick lenses of his glasses. "Well, Lyda," he said, "we pulled it off."

"Yes, David," said Lyda Southard. "We pulled it off."

Chapter Fourteen

The banshee wail of the prison siren sundered the quiet Idaho night. Running boots on cobblestones echoed throughout the compound of the Idaho State Penitentiary. In his bedroom, Warden Thomas leaped to his feet, reached for his trousers. In a sickening flash he knew he was in trouble. Having a jailbreak was hardly the way to start a new custodial career.

As Thomas rushed into his office, he was met by a guard with a rifle in the crook of his arm. "Escape from the women's quarters," the guard exclaimed. "I was just making my rounds outside the wall when I spotted a dangling rope."

"Come with me!" barked the warden, heading out the door.

The two men shouldered their way through the milling throng that had gathered, the scene underscored by the wail of the siren.

Minutes later the men entered the women's cell block. A flashlight revealed two women standing in their cells, their white knuckles gripping the bars, their faces thrust through them. Thomas knew from the morning report that there were three prisoners in the women's cells. So far two were accounted for. The warden quickly strode over to the cell at the end that had been occupied for almost ten years by the prison's headliner inmate. Lyda Southard must be sleeping through the hubbub, he thought, as her cot showed the outlines of her figure. Thomas called to her. There was no response. And then the swinging flashlight beam showed that one of the bars on Lyda's window was missing.

Cursing, the warden ordered the guard to open her cell. The two men rushed in, pulled the covers back on Lyda's bed. There was no female body. Bundles of clothes had been arranged under the coverlet to resemble a sleeping person.

Turning their attention to the window, the men saw that the removal of one of the bars provided egress through the window for a medium-sized person. Furthermore, the outside screen that covered the window had been propped open.

There was no doubt about it. One of Idaho State Penitentiary's most deadly criminals had escaped. Right under the nose of its new warden, E. R. Thomas.

A human net was spread out over the surrounding countryside to pick up the daring fugitive. All trains were checked. Off-duty guards formed a posse to search the nearby fields. Motorcycle cops zoomed up and down the roadways, stopping anything that moved.

It was easy for Warden Thomas to reconstruct Lyda's carefully planned and executed escape. An examination of the bar found in her cell showed it had been sawed apart some time before. The sawed-off end was rusty. The inmate had been able to do the job without detection because the bar had been loose in its sockets, and could be raised slightly. Lyda had been able to raise the bar into its upper socket, saw through it close to the lower windowsill, then drop it back into its lower socket. In that way, the periodic inspection of her cell disclosed nothing.

When the escapee was ready to leave, she had simply raised the bar, pulled the bottom part inward, and lowered it down over the windowsill. This had left an opening large enough to crawl through.

Footprints outside the cell window revealed the inmate had walked across the soft ground to the rosebushes. There she had disentangled two rose trellises consisting of long iron bars welded together by crossbars. Lyda had obviously fitted the trellises together and made the thin but durable ladder that now leaned against the inside wall of the women's enclosure.

Near the ladder was a low wooden bench. On the bench were a basket and two wooden fruit boxes loaded with stones. Using the bench as an anchor, one end of a garden hose had been secured to the bench. The other end of the hose extended up and over the prison wall. But the hose was not long enough to reach the bottom of the other side, so Lyda had braided a rope of stripped blankets and her mattress cover to tie to the end of the hose. This had enabled her to reach the ground on the outside of the fence.

The spot where she had chosen to go over the top was in the shadow of the bulging corner of the wall, beyond which was a tree. Its heavy foliage had kept her in shadows as she had climbed down on the outside. Her footprints were followed across the field and into a copse of trees, where they disappeared into tire marks. The tire marks led to the road, where they were no longer distinguishable in the dusty ruts of the roadway.

Warden Thomas leaned back in his desk chair, his eyes fixed on a crack in the ceiling. His mind raced backwards, envisioning the events that had led to Lyda Southard's escape. He saw her chunky figure, her soft blue eyes, as she moved purposefully around her courtyard picking up stones, dropping them into the containers that would act as counterbalance to her weight when she shinnied over the wall. Indeed, he himself had said some kind words to Lyda about keeping the courtyard so tidy and pretty. Little did he realize this comely, demure lady was not nearly as interested in beautifying the grounds as she was in engineering a diabolical escape plot that would have challenged Sherlock Holmes himself.

But who was Lyda's accomplice? Reason suggested that it was probably someone Lyda had met during her prison tenure. Thomas racked his brain. The rose trellises had to be a clue. They had been cleverly designed and manufactured by someone in prison. This should be easy to track down.

Searching records and querying guards, Warden Thomas soon came up with the likely accomplice. The trellises had been constructed nearly a year before by a trusty named David Minton. Minton was employed in the prison machine-shop.

Reviewing Minton's records, the warden found himself staring at the photo of a middle-aged man with a shock of dark hair graying at the temples. Loose-lipped and with a cast in one eye, Minton could hardly be called handsome. He had served a short term for petty forgery and had chalked up a record in Colorado as a car thief. On the outside he had earned his living serving the incongruous trades of machinist and trap-drummer.

Studying the photo, Warden Thomas divined that Minton was a man who could be easily swayed. It seemed apparent that Lyda, the seductress, who had duped other men in other ways and days, could easily have made a pawn of the nearsighted machinist.

Following up this lead, the warden's interviews of guards and inmates disclosed additional facts. The interest of Minton in Lyda, and vice-versa, had been one of those happenings that go on in prison despite the closest surveillance. Tedious investigation disclosed that the trusties and the women prisoners knew of the relationship. The warden's crackdown also turned up the fact that Minton had made a passkey so that he could enter the women's quarters. He had been known to visit Lyda on more than one occasion.

At a briefing with the Boise lawmen, Warden Thomas recapped his latest conclusions. "Trusty David Minton got her out of here," Thomas said, "there's no question about it. Minton was released two weeks ago. He evidently procured a car, and he and Lyda planned the right moment for the prison break.

"We must find out where he got the car, get a description of it. As I see it, these two will do one of three things. They'll either lie low here in Boise until the search has died down, then make a break for it. Or they might try hiding in the nearby hills for a while. But my guess is that they started driving hard last night and they won't stop until they've got as many miles as possible between them and this prison."

One of the police officers nodded. "They only had an hour's start when you turned in the alarm," he said. "I'm surprised we haven't picked them up already. We'll have them before the day is over if they stick to the roads."

"I wouldn't count on it," said the warden. "We're dealing with a couple of slippery customers here. But there is one thing on our side. There's a notation in Minton's record that he's nearsighted and wears very thick glasses. He seems to be accident-prone, having had several auto crashes. If he's doing the driving now, he'll undoubtedly be driving fast, and we just might have an accident waiting to happen."

The warden pulled out a bag of Bull Durham, shaped a cigarette paper in his hand, and rolled himself a cigarette. Then he looked around at the grim faces of the police officers. "But we can't count on them crashing. Lyda might do most of the driving. And she knows how to handle a car as well as a man. Better, in this case. And watch yourselves, gentlemen. Minton shouldn't be dangerous, but Lyda has to be desperate to do what she did. And she's canny. She might put up one helluva fight if she's cornered." The warden stood, signifying that the meeting was over.

After the men had filed out, Thomas sagged down into his chair. He picked up the prison photos of his two fugitives, studied them through his cigarette smoke. What odd bedmates prison can produce. A crafty murderess and a nearsighted petty thief. Was it really a romance on Lyda's part? Or was Minton merely being used? Even in prison this Lorelei had been able to seduce a man into doing her bidding.

The warden's thoughts turned to his own problems. He knew before the day was over his political opponents would have a field day with Lyda's escape. They would say her getaway was due to his carelessness; they would demand an investigation. He had come to the prison only a month before, after seven years of service as the state game warden. The prison had been unfamiliar to him, but he had worked day and night trying to improve conditions. And now this had to happen.

The warden knew that he would never get a good night's sleep until he had recaptured his notorious prisoner.

The days passed, but still no word of Lyda's capture. The Boise police and the county sheriff's posse worked tirelessly, combing the desert and mountain lands in the vicinity without so much as a clue. The criticism that Warden Thomas had expected, however, began arriving in abundance. The press had its field day, his political opponents smacked their lips.

But as a result of the front-page newspaper publicity, information began pouring in to the warden's office. Several people reported seeing a man answering Minton's description on the eastern outskirts of Boise near the prison. He was sitting in an old Hupmobile roadster.

This clue developed another lead. It was learned that a 1921 Hupmobile roadster had been sighted near a bridge, just before dark, a few hours before the female inmate's escape. A search of local car dealers disclosed that a Hupmobile roadster bearing a California license, 3-D-2620, had been sold by the Cranston Automobile Company of Boise on April 17 to a man resembling Minton. The price paid was fifty-five dollars.

The date of the sale was the day after Minton's parole from prison.

When this information was released, the local police were flooded with calls. A Boise sheep rancher named Sam Ballantyne explained that he had been stopped by a lone woman on the road after Lyda's escape. The woman had waved to him asking for a ride, but he had refused. Police found the woman. She was not Lyda.

Several townsfolk told of hearing an airplane circling low over the city on the night of Lyda's escape. The motor had been heard to stop, then to start up again a few minutes later. This indicated a landing and a take-off. It was suggested that Lyda and Minton had chartered a plane and headed for Mexico. Police officials hurried to an old, unused airport on the outskirts of Boise. They found car tracks and the skid marks of a plane. But where was the car?

A former police official, who had known Lyda, declared he had seen her on the streets of Spokane.

The clues continued pouring in to the *Statesman* and the *Capital News*. One writer said Lyda had ditched the sedan in lava rock and was wandering around in Lost Valley. Another citizen advised finding Dead Shot Reed and following him to the end of the trail. There among the pine-clad mountains would be found either Lyda or the pot of gold.

Sunset Slavens of Pistil City said she was holed up in the mountains south of Twin Falls. Women wrote in taking Lyda's side, urging the nasty old lawmen to leave her be. A hot tip in the desert north of Idaho Falls caused a red-faced posse to flush a Cyprian carrying the Good Word to Basque sheepherders.

Unfortunately, all of these hot tips fizzled out when checked by the authorities. Warden Thomas was becoming increasingly despondent.

Then came a lead that seemed to promise something more. It was especially valuable, as it appeared to jibe with some secret information the warden had unearthed concerning Lyda. The new lead came in the form of a letter to Warden Thomas from a Robert Fulton, student at Gooding College, Idaho. The letter read:

> Last April 18 I was hitch-hiking from the college to Twin Falls when picked up by a man driving an old Hupmobile roadster. This man answered the description I have seen published of David Minton. We ran out of gas at the Rim-to-Rim Bridge, and as we were walking across he mentioned to me that in a few weeks he would be down at the Royal Gorge in Colorado. He also mentioned that he was going to return to Boise that night, saying "I've got a date with a little woman."
>
> At the Twin Falls Post Office he asked me to call for mail at the General Delivery window for H. O. Mills. I got a letter and he opened it and showed me two traveler's checks of some sort. One was for $30 and the other for $53. In spite of the fact that this man gave me the name of H. O. Mills, I feel sure he is this man Minton. He said he had paid $55 for the car the day before. It was a Hupmobile with a California license.

Warden Thomas pored over this letter in his office. The secret information he possessed seemed to check with the letter.

Prisoners in the Idaho penitentiary were allowed to cash checks or express money orders on such funds as they may have had or accumulated in prison. This money was kept on deposit with the prison authorities, and the spending of it was not questioned.

Checking back on Lyda's activities, Thomas discovered that about ten days prior to her escape she had drawn up two orders payable to H. O. Mills, who had been Lyda's attorney at the time of her trial. But a check with Mills disclosed that he had never received the letters or money orders.

Evidently Lyda had meant the money to reach Minton's hands. It was also discovered that Minton had purchased an extensive amount of provisions and a camping outfit in Boise just before Lyda's getaway. Neither of the two checks, however, had been cashed in Boise or Twin Falls.

Warden Thomas rolled himself a cigarette as he mulled this. Then he came up with a plan. He decided not to stop payment on the checks, but to let them ride. The locales in which they were cashed would be clues to the route Lyda and Minton were taking.

As the days rolled by, the warden and the police concluded that the fugitives were not hiding in Boise. Lyda and her nearsighted love-interest must have eluded all watchers and slipped out of the state. Or they might be hiding somewhere in the wild desert or mountain country. This idea seemed remote, as the weather was still cold and the snow was deep in the mountain passes, even though it was May. However, this possibility was strengthened by a mysterious tip that had reached *The Idaho Statesman*. The clue was in the form of a letter and a map:

"If you have any interest in the capture of Lyda Southard," said the anonymous correspondent, "get two intelligent men — men who know the desert. Have these men go to Twin Falls and then follow this diagram."

The map pictured a trail winding from an X marking Twin Falls. The trail wound north and east to a camp in the desert, then turned off south and east to a place marked "hiding place." This place was indicated by a circle.

"The men who take up this trail must not be ordinary policemen," the writer continued, "but men who know and are able to read the language of the desert. Lyda Southard will be found in this place if the right men are sent.

"I sign only Circle C."

The signature was a large capital C containing a smaller c inside of it.

Warden Thomas had little faith in anonymous letters, but feeling he should leave no stone unturned, he briefed the searching lawmen on the message. A posse was formed to explore the south Idaho desert and hill country. Another group even penetrated the arid Utah desert country near the Great Salt Lake.

But all searchers returned empty-handed, thus confirming Thomas's gut feeling that Lyda Southard was not the type who would take to the hills. Her past life had indicated her craving for the gayer life of towns and cities. And men. She was not about to escape from prison only to hole up in some isolated ravine.

Warden Thomas had been waiting impatiently for one of the express money orders mailed by Lyda to Twin Falls to be cashed. On the tenth of May his agonizing wait was over. An express money order had been cashed at a restaurant in Rawlins, Wyoming. Thomas's hopes soared.

Word was immediately flashed to the Rawlins police chief to search for the fleeing couple. But the answer came back that the couple had vanished after spending only one night in town.

Thomas called his men in for a briefing. Pointing to a map of the Rocky Mountain states pinned on the wall, he used it to illustrate the fugitives' possible course. "That's the route they took," he said, running his finger across the map from Boise to Twin Falls to Ogden, Utah, to Rawlins. "Rawlins sits on the southern part of Wyoming near the Colorado line. I've got a plug of chewing tobacco that says they're heading back toward Minton's old stomping ground — Colorado. Minton has relatives living back there, but the police haven't been able to locate them." He tapped the map on the state of Colorado. "Yes, sir, men. That's where we're going to find our pair of lovebirds."

A few more days passed, then another money order surfaced. Thomas's heart nearly went into fibrillation when he saw that his theory had been correct. The second express money order had been cashed at Fort Collins, Colorado.

Thomas could smell victory. His escapee would soon be back in her cage along with her accomplice.

The Fort Collins police scoured the town; every police chief in Colorado was on the lookout. Even the secret operatives of the United States Department of Justice Bureau of Investigation were taking up the search.

Yet, once again Lyda had outwitted the police. She and Minton had been able to slip through the tight net that had been spun around them. The police and federal operatives were armed with photos and a full description of the pair, but there were two factors that loomed in favor of the outlaws. The prison picture of Lyda had been taken years before and it showed her glum-faced and without makeup. It made her appear almost ugly. Minton's photo had appeared without his glasses, making an entirely different impression than the man with two headlamp lenses covering his face.

Lyda had changed considerably since her prison photo. She was now thirty-nine years old. She had put on some weight and now wore glasses. Also, the somber-eyed prison photo did not do justice to the true character of the murderess. She was generally smiling, jolly, and exuding good cheer.

All of these points were definitely in the favor of the female temptress and her escort.

While Warden Thomas spent his time worrying and fending off the assaults of his political opponents, an interesting event was transpiring in Longmont, Colorado.

A woman left a drugstore and slipped her purchase into her handbag. It was a small, black bottle emblazoned with a skull and crossbones. The woman walked along the street with her handbag tucked under her arm, her mouth pressed into a grim straight line.

She went up the front steps of the city hall, passed several policemen, then walked along a corridor to a room where a man was being questioned. The suspect was being grilled about an automobile accident. The woman stood in the background, silently watching the man. The man answered the policeman's questions in a matter-of-fact voice. Finally the official said, "Well, you may go."

The man turned, went to the rear of the room, and he and the woman left the building together. The man was wearing thick glasses, the brim of his hat down over his eyes. When they were a block away from the city hall the woman relaxed. "That was a close call," she whispered. "I never should have let you take the car."

"It's that damned car," said the man. "It just don't want to steer right."

"It steers fine. From now on, I'll do the driving." She glared at him. "If you had to run into somebody, why did you pick someone who worked in the police station?"

"Mr. Layne was a nice man. He agreed to accept three dollars cash for damage to his car. I paid him."

"Good. Then you didn't have to fill out a police report?"

"No. All I did was sign my name to an accident report."

She looked at him incredulously. "You signed your real name to a police form?"

He looked sheepish. "I'm sorry, Lyda. I guess I did it without thinking."

"I guess you did. I thought you might have learned something after your accident in Fort Collins. It's a good thing I handled that accident. Or we'd both be back in Boise by this time."

"I'm truly sorry, Lyda. It won't happen again."

"You are right there, David. It won't happen again."

Chapter Fifteen

Days passed into weeks; weeks passed into months. Still no hide nor hair of Lyda Southard or David Minton. Warden Thomas, the United States Bureau of Investigation, and the police chiefs of the Rocky Mountain states were convinced that the fugitives were somewhere in that vast territory. But no law officer had been able to put his finger on them.

Warden Thomas spent many a sleepless night as his very job hinged, to a large extent, on the recapture of his most notorious prisoner. His political foes were beginning to turn their large guns on him.

He tried putting himself in the shoes of Lyda, and then in those of her accomplice. Were they still together, or had they split up? Would Lyda slip back into her old ways and plan further murders? Indeed, was David Minton still alive and kicking?

As he rolled and tossed in his bed, the warden devised new ways to effect her capture. He ached to go out and join the far-flung hunt himself. But that was not in the cards. He had to stay home and oversee the guarding of the other prison inmates. If another prison escape happened, his fat would really be in the fire. He knew he would not get a good night's sleep until the handcuffs had been snapped around Lyda Southard's wrists again.

Thomas had gone over every existing record of Lyda — including her preliminary trial and incarceration — searching for clues. During his research he had come to know the man most responsible for the murderess's arrest, Deputy Sheriff Virgil Ormsby, who had figured so prominently in the woman's past. The warden was beginning to feel a kinship with the little bulldog who had tracked her down. Indeed, they had both been outwitted by this wisp of a woman who had led them each on a wild goose chase.

139

Happily, before he died, Ormsby had had the last laugh, seeing his quarry in prison. Thomas sincerely hoped he would be as fortunate.

Fall painted the trees in the Rocky Mountain canyons with its colors of gold and brown. Then came the deep snows. Had Lyda Southard and David Minton stepped off the face of the earth? In spite of the unflagging efforts of lawmen from several states, no trace of the escapees had been found.

Then on the night of May 3, almost one year to the day since the prison break, something happened in Denver, Colorado. A newspaperman named Wallis Reef walked into the office of Denver Police Chief G. T. Clark.

"Chief," said Reef, pushing his hat back on his head, "I just received a tip from one of my informants. It concerns this man David Minton you've been searching for. Interested?"

The chief's feet came off his desk to hit the floor with a bang. "Let's have it, Reef."

"Well, sir, it seems Minton has some relatives living in Erie, Colorado. My tip is that Minton himself has been visiting them in Erie. According to my fairly reliable source, he's there now."

"Good news!" The chief's eyes brightened. "I'll send two of my boys down there and see if they can snare him. Any sign of the woman?"

"The informant didn't say. But I'd like to go down to Erie with your men. If they make the pinch, I should get the story."

"Deal," said the chief, picking up his phone. He made a quick call, then two men entered the room. The chief spoke to the correspondent. "Reef, shake hands with Detectives Henry Genty and J. Sherman Turner. Men, this is the reporter who gave us the tip. Wallis Reef." The men shook hands.

"Genty and Turner," said the chief, "have been on this case since we got the word our fugitives might be in Colorado. Genty arrested Minton in 1916 in Denver for car theft."

"Yep," said Genty, a jowly, heavy-set man with a large, commanding nose. "I know our nearsighted ex-con fairly well."

The chief explained the situation and Genty and Turner nodded. "Erie is about forty miles from here," said Turner, another beefy man who could have been a wrestler. His homburg was cocked down over one eye. "We can drive there in an hour. If Minton's in town, we'll get him."

The newspaperman studied the two detectives. These hefty men could have comprised the whole backfield of a major football team. Reef shuddered as he thought of what a felon must feel when he came up against either of these men.

An hour later it was close to midnight as the police car sped into the town of Erie. "I have an idea," said Reef. "As a reporter, I know a few people here. Suppose you let me make some inquiries. I'll find out where Minton's relatives live."

The detectives agreed. They parked the police car on a side street and let Reef out. Fifteen minutes later he returned. "I've got the address. I'll give directions as we go along."

The car started up with Turner at the wheel. They drove through the dark night, Reef squinting at the street signs. Five minutes later the news-man ordered a stop. The three men got quietly out of the car.

"That should be the house," said Reef, pointing. "Minton's bedroom is on the first floor."

"Okay," said Genty. "Turner and I will take over. You stay back out of the way. I'd hate to have a member of the press corps hurt on our watch."

"Yes, sir." Reef got behind the two men as they approached the dark house. "If Minton's here, that should be his bedroom there at the front of the house."

Genty drew a flashlight, Turner produced his gun. The window before them was dark. The shade had been raised. Genty directed his flashlight into the room, snapped it on. The spot of light showed an empty chair, then a bed. The bed was empty. The coverlet was unruffled. The bed had not been slept in. The spot went around the room, across the floor, over the chairs and bureau, along the walls. No signs of recent occupancy.

Reef swore. "The whole damned house is empty."

"Luck of the draw," said Genty. "Let's stay here in town, get some shut-eye, and query the neighbors in the morning."

The other men agreed.

By noon the next day, the three men had turned up some very valuable information. It was definite that Minton had arrived recently in town, accompanied by a woman. The two had departed a couple of days before.

But who was the woman? And where had they gone? None of the townspeople seemed to know. Nor could they identify her as Lyda from her prison picture. Genty and Turner asked local police officials to keep a sharp lookout for the two, then headed back toward Denver with Reef.

"Well," said Genty, as the car sped back toward the Colorado metropolis, "That was a good tip, Reef, but we didn't get it early enough. Those two may be back in Denver by now."

"I'm as disappointed as you are, gentlemen," said the reporter. "We just blew a great story all to hell."

For the next week the two sleuths redoubled their efforts to pick up some sign of the fugitives in the city. Their energies produced nothing. Discouraged, they decided that their premise had been wrong, and that Lyda and Minton had gone on to some other town.

The months of May and June were marked off on the calendar of the increasingly frustrated Warden Thomas. And then, on July first, came an interesting report from the detective team of Genty and Turner.

The two detectives had been in the Bertillon room of the Denver police station looking up an accident report on a routine case. Going through the stack of old reports, Turner had suddenly let out an oath. "Goddam! Would you believe this?"

Genty peered over his shoulder. The object of Turner's consternation was an accident card with the name of David Minton, and an address on South Logan Street. The report, several months old, contained the circumstances of an accident in which Minton had crashed into another car.

"Think of that old boy getting away with this, and no one in the police station recognizing the name," growled Genty. "Talk about being shot in the ass with luck! That guy is covered with horseshoes. Let's get our butts out to that Logan Street address."

Ten minutes later the two sleuths had parked their car on South Logan Street and were walking toward the house number given on the accident report. It was an unpretentious home set back from the street. The window shades were drawn. The two detectives went to the front door and rang the bell. No one answered. They rang again. The house was as quiet as a tomb. On the third ring a woman came out of the house next door.

"That house isn't occupied," said the woman.

"No?" questioned Genty, turning to the woman. "Then perhaps you can answer some questions for us." Genty flashed his badge. "We're the police."

The woman came over to the porch, wiping her hands on her apron. "Excuse my mess. I'm making pies." She presented a cluster of floury fingers to the two men. "Always willing to help the police. What can I tell you?"

The men were quickly filled in on the fact that the house's occupants had moved out recently. They had given their names as Rains. Mr. and Mrs. David Rains.

"Rains," repeated Genty. "What did they look like?"

"I never saw Mrs. Rains with her hat off," the woman answered. "She was of medium height, and he was a man of maybe fifty . . . and wore glasses. Real thick glasses. He had gray hair. Seemed to squint a lot."

"You don't know where they've moved?" asked Genty.

"No." The woman shook her head. "They didn't confide in me." She moved in closer to the two men and spoke in a low voice. "If you ask me, they weren't very sociable. They never did invite me into their house."

"They made a mistake there," said Turner. "I'll bet you make a mean pie."

"That I do. Make a pretty good apple pie, if I do say so myself." She smiled up at the men. "Say, would you boys care for a piece? Right out of the oven?"

The detectives reluctantly demurred, thanked her, then wandered around the side of the house. They found a back window that was unlocked. Raising it, they climbed inside. They searched the house from top to bottom. They uncovered nothing. The house had obviously been rented furnished, with the most rudimentary furnishings. It appeared to have been thoroughly cleaned, leaving not so much as a soiled wastebasket. Discouraged, the two men clambered back out of the window and began a cursory search of the grounds.

Turner spotted a crumpled piece of paper in the backyard that had blown up against the back fence. It was dirty and gray from exposure to the elements, but he picked it up, smoothed it out in his hand. Then he let out a yelp to his partner. "Genty. Come here!"

Turner's sidekick joined him, looked down at his open palm. "What have we here?"

"It's a receipted bill for milk delivered to Mr. David Rains at this address."

"Hot damn! This just might be the break we need."

"Let's hope so. We'll check with this milk company. If the Rainses are still taking milk from this dairy, they should have their new address."

Genty clapped his partner on the back. "Good work, detective. We're gonna nail those wise-asses yet."

A half hour later Genty and Turner were in the milk company's office, grilling the clerk. "The Rainses moved to 322 West Second Avenue," said the clerk, looking up from her record book. "That address is still good. We delivered milk there this morning."

The two men exchanged glances, then Genty reached over and patted the surprised clerk on her cheek. "Thanks for your help," he said, as the two men headed for the door. "Thank you very much."

It was late in the afternoon when the two detectives again parked their car in a Denver neighborhood. The house bearing the given address showed obvious signs of occupancy. The shades were up, flowers near the house had been freshly watered.

As the two men approached the house, Genty stopped and huddled with Turner. "Let's block all exits," he said. "Why don't you go around to the rear and come in the back door. We don't want our birds to back-door us and get away this time. And keep a hand on your gun. I don't know about Minton, but if our lady Bluebeard is cornered, she just might try anything."

"Good plan," said Turner, starting toward the rear of the house. Genty gave his partner time to get into place at the back door, then he sauntered up the sidewalk and stopped in front of the house. He walked up on the porch as quietly as his squeaky shoes would permit and paused at the door. He waited a moment, listening. No sound. He slowly turned the doorknob. It was unlocked. He silently let himself in.

He found himself in a narrow hallway. Straight ahead was a stairway leading upstairs. At left was a door leading to a parlor, and at the end of the hall was another door. Both doors were closed. Genty softly opened the door on the left. The front parlor was empty. He closed it, and was about to walk down the hallway when the door at the end opened.

A woman stood there, her eyes suddenly wide with fright. She was a youngish, dark-haired woman, fairly tall. Genty walked toward her slowly, his hands at his sides, his piercing gaze taking in her every detail. The woman backed away from him, her mouth opening as if she were about to scream.

"Don't be afraid," said Genty quietly. "I'm not going to hurt you. I'm not an intruder. Everything's going to be just fine."

The women backed away from him, her hand covering her mouth. Her terror had robbed her of speech, her eyes bugged in their sockets.

In the dining room Genty stopped. Behind the woman an open doorway led to the kitchen, and through the back door screen he could see a man sitting on the back porch reading a newspaper.

Genty's pace quickened. The woman ran before him, and out onto the back porch. As she cried out, the man on the porch chair dropped his paper. Genty reached for his gun, then looked down into the startled eyes of the man in the chair.

"Hello, Dave," said Genty softly. "Long time no see."

Minton's mouth dropped open. The fugitive could only stare in silence, his vocal cords paralyzed.

The woman began to cry, clapping her hands over her face. The back gate creaked, and out of the corner of his eye Genty saw his partner push it open and enter, his gun drawn.

Minton gulped, trying to summon saliva to his dry mouth. The newspaper fluttered in his hands as he finally found words. "So we meet again, Officer Genty. What's up?"

Genty smiled grimly. Turner moved onto the back porch and stood near the woman, holstering his weapon. Then Genty said quietly, "I think you know what's up, Minton." He looked over at the woman.

This gesture brought Minton scrambling to his feet. He raised a protesting hand as he faced his adversary. "Henry, you got this all wrong. I'll bet you thought I'd be with Lyda Southard. Well, you're wrong. This woman isn't Lyda. You can see that for yourself. I don't know anything about Lyda. And I had nothing to do with her getaway. I never saw her after I left the Idaho pen."

Genty waited patiently for Minton to finish. Then he pulled out from his pocket the police bulletin photograph of Lyda Southard. The detective's heart sank as he saw there was no resemblance between the two women. Even if Lyda had tried to change her looks, she could not have made herself taller or more youthful. Nor were the features the same. Genty shrugged in disappointment.

"Okay, Minton. You may be telling the truth about this young lady here. We'll go down to the station and sort it all out."

Warden Thomas glared at the yellow telegram in his hand that had just crackled over the telegraph wires from Denver.

DAVID MINTON ARRESTED HERE TODAY. ADVISE. CLARK

A gleam of hope came to the warden's eyes as he reread the message from the Denver chief of police. He reached for the phone and quickly made arrangements to fly to Denver.

It had been a long night. The grilling interrogation by Police Chief Clark and Detectives Genty and Turner was taking its toll. The gnarled and homely figure of David Minton slumped in the chair in front of the glaring spotlight made feeble by the thick cigar and cigarette smoke fouling the small room.

"Now, Dave," said Genty for the fiftieth time, "tell us where she is. We're going to get her anyway. It would be to your advantage to come clean. We've released your girl friend, now why not cooperate with us? Turn Lyda in and get the breaks for yourself."

Minton squinted at them through watering eyes. "I'd tell you if I knew." His voice was husky, shaking. "I don't know. That's straight. I admit I helped her on the getaway. I admit we traveled around together for a couple months. But then we separated. She gave me the air. She said she wanted to be on her own, so she took a train and left. Then I found this new woman. I like her better. I don't ever want to see Lyda again. I tell you I'm all washed up with that woman. I have no idea where she might be."

Leaning back in his chair, Detective Turner's eyes lit up. "You say Lyda took the train?"

Minton shot his hand up. "As God is my witness. She got on the train in Cheyenne. I came down here by myself."

"Where was her destination when she boarded the train?"

Minton shook his head. "I don't know. And didn't care. I was just glad to see her out of my life."

"Are you saying," grilled Genty, "that you weren't with her in Erie, your hometown, the latter part of last April?"

"I was not." Minton's eyes focused on the ceiling. "I was with someone else."

Someone else," echoed Turner. "Would that be the lady we found you with at the house?"

"No. That was a different woman."

"A different woman. You're quite a ladies' man, aren't you, Minton?"

A half-grin toyed with Minton's lips. "I seem to be attractive to women, yes."

And so the battle of wits and endurance waged far into the night. No amount of grilling seemed to shake Minton's confession. They managed to poke a few holes in the fugitive's story, yet there was the possibility that, by and large, he might be telling the truth. When the first rays of dawn began to finger the floor of the smoke-filled room, the police officers were ready to suspend their grilling of the man who had fallen asleep in his chair.

Genty reached up and turned off the spotlight that had been glaring in the victim's face. He turned to his fellow officers. "Is this guy telling the truth? Do you think he really doesn't know where Lyda is hiding?"

Turner and Clark shrugged, threw their coats over their shoulders, and headed for the door. "It beats the hell out of me" said Turner.

Warden Thomas sat next to the window in the airplane that was whisking him to Denver. He was not accustomed to flying, and the anxiety showed in his face as he looked out of the plane's window at the mountain and desert country speeding by below his feet. Shoulders hunched forward, fingers clenched, he thought about the recent events.

Lyda had been gone now for three days shy of fourteen months. He was still hanging on to his job, but only by a thread. He would not be able to redeem himself until he again had this ulcerating woman behind bars. At least they had finally found her accomplice. Thomas did not care all that much about Minton, but he could be a tool in the recapture of his number one quarry. He was very much looking forward to meeting this man in the flesh.

Thomas felt a queasiness in the pit of his stomach as the engines increased their power to start their climb over the Colorado Rockies.

God! The things he had to do in the interests of law and order.

The grilling of David Minton had been resumed by officers Genty, Turner, and Clark. Chief Clark's voice was low, almost pleading. "For Christ's sake, Minton. That Southard woman is dangerous. She could be slowly poisoning someone while you're sitting there. Do you realize what this means? If you do know anything, come across."

Minton stared at his inquisitioner with vacuous eyes. "I wish you gents would just let me get some sleep."

"Sleep!" roared Genty, trying a different tack. "Sleep is what Lyda's husbands get. Sleep through all eternity. Come on, Minton. Level with us."

Minton's eyes curtained. "I want to see my sister."

"Your sister?" asked Clark.

"My sister. She lives here in Denver."

Genty and Turner exchanged glances. "What is the address of your sister, Minton?" asked Turner.

"If I give you the address, will you send for her?"

"We'll be glad to," said Clark. "The police are more than happy to cooperate with you. Perhaps you might consider repaying the favor. What say you, Minton?"

"I say I want to go to sleep." His chin fell on his chest, and within minutes deep rales issued from Minton's chest.

A woman dressed in a smock stood before the bureau in her bedroom. She looked at her reflection in the mirror, then made a slight face as if unimpressed with the image. She fluffed her hair, smoothed down her bodice, and opened one of the bureau drawers.

She felt around in a nest of undergarments, finally found what she was seeking. She pulled out a small black bottle. The bottle bore a skull and crossbones. She stared at the bottle for a moment, then looked at her visage in the mirror. She shook her head, placed the vial back in the bureau drawer, turned quickly and left the room.

She went into the nearby bedroom where a small boy lay ill in bed. A man was standing at the foot of the bed regarding the boy with pained, anxious eyes.

"How is he?" the woman asked.

The man shook his head, answered in a barely discernible whisper. "He's not doing well. I just don't understand it. He seems to get better, then suddenly he takes a turn for the worse."

The woman looked up into the man's face with level, dispassionate eyes. "What did the doctor say?"

"He says he thinks Buddy might have been poisoned."

"Poisoned?" At the word, the woman seemed to flinch.

"He says Buddy must have eaten something bad and he can't seem to get the poison out of the child's system."

The woman put her hand on the man's shoulder and gave him a slight smile. "Don't you worry. My nursing will pull him through. I'm sure."

The man gave her a weak, reassuring smile and left the room. The woman gave the boy an indifferent glance, then turned to stare after the man. Her dull, flat eyes were suddenly invaded by a bright, hard gleam. She moved slowly toward the sick child.

David Minton's sister was brought to police headquarters by one of Chief Clark's patrolmen. They were sequestered at Minton's request. Nearly half an hour later she left to return home.

In the detectives' assembly room, Genty and Turner conferred. "Do you think Minton's lying?" asked Turner bluntly. "Do you think he really knows where Lyda is?"

Genty shook his head. "I wish to hell I knew. David Minton's a weird codger. He just might have some misguided sense of loyalty to the old girl. Let's give him one more whirl."

The woman had traded her house frock for a black dress. She hurried through the Denver streets, walking rapidly, an intense look on her face.

The July night was cool and mild, the hour was so late that few people were stirring in the streets. The woman seemed to be walking on cat's feet, moving like a wraith, never pausing until she reached the sidewalk leading to the front door of a dark house. She took this walk, mounted the porch, and looking both ways, silently entered.

Chapter Sixteen

"Hello, Warden," said David Minton, as Warden Thomas entered his cell. "How they hangin'?"

The warden sat down on the bunk beside his prisoner, studying the homely face of the fugitive. It was the first time they had met in person. "Hello, Minton."

"Nice day."

"Very nice day on the outside." Thomas took off his hat. "You should be out there enjoying it, instead of being locked up in here."

"I'm ready. The chow in here stinks."

The questioning began. With disarming candor, Minton repeated the story he had given to the Denver police. Two hours later Warden Thomas left the cell, walked to the office of Chief G. T. Clark.

"Any luck?" asked the chief.

"Struck out," said Thomas, taking a chair in front of the chief's desk.

"You know, I thought we were pretty good at interrogating. Detectives Genty, Turner, and I have all taken a crack at him. Either Minton's telling the truth, or he's putting on one hell of a show."

Thomas bit the end off a cigar. "Minton's lying."

"That's what we think."

Thomas opened the drawstring on the pouch of Bull Durham, shook some tobacco into the cigarette paper in his hand, and rolled a cigarette with one hand while closing the drawstring with his teeth. He skated a kitchen match across his bottom and lit the cigarette. "I'm sure of it. And there's one way to make him crack. Extradite him. I'll take him back to Idaho. When he's back in the Big House, facing another long-term prison

149

sentence, he'll talk. You can bet on it."

"You're probably right." Chief Clark swiveled back and forth in his chair. "You got to hand it to Lyda Southard. That ole gal's sure got something. Wherever she is, she's still got Minton by the balls. She seems to have some kind of hypnotic power over men."

"Or maybe she's got some kind of hypnotic power in her bloomers. Whatever it is, it sure seems to work."

"Amen to that. Well, Warden, we'll start extradition papers at once."

"Thanks, Chief. I think it's the best plan."

David Minton was not all that excited about returning to Boise, Idaho. With the help of an attorney, he managed to do a good deal of foot-dragging before the extradition papers were finally signed, sealed, and delivered. During this time he was visited daily by his sister. The police questioned her, too, but again ran up against a brick wall.

On July 15, 1932, Minton was led from his cell and delivered into the custody of Warden Thomas. A short time later the two men boarded the train for Idaho.

Sitting stiffly in a Pullman compartment, the keen-eyed warden and the handcuffed, nondescript, gray-haired ex-convict faced each other. Minton was in an ebullient mood, being out of the depressing jail for the first time in weeks. He watched the mountainous scenery fly by, his watery, nearsighted eyes blinking against the sun.

Warden Thomas stared at his ward, trying to enter his mind. What was this man thinking? Was he telling the truth? Or was he protecting one of the most enigmatic women in history? Time would tell. Those forbidding gray stone walls of the Idaho penitentiary had cracked more than one man. Men far more dangerous and determined than this mild-mannered Milquetoast with the thick-lensed glasses.

Or were they?

The woman in the demure housedress put down the morning paper. She again glanced at the front page headlines blaring the fact that David Minton had been extradited to Idaho.

She went to her bedroom and shut the door. She paced the floor, deep in thought. Then she suddenly stopped, staring at the bureau.

She went over to the chest, pulled out the top drawer, picked up the small black bottle, and slipped it into her purse.

Then she put on her hat and went downstairs.

The turnkey frisked the prisoner. Then David Minton was ushered through the four doors — only one of which could be unlocked at any one time — and returned to the blockhouse he had known so well. Here he would be held to await his trial for abetting Lyda Southard's escape.

Warden Thomas watched Minton like a hawk, giving him no rest, summoning him from time to time to answer more questions. He was intent on wearing down this pawn in Lyda's great chess game.

The evening of the first day it became apparent that the warden's psychology was beginning to pay off. Minton seemed to grow more wan and nervous with the passing of each hour. Well into the midnight hours, Minton made a surprise announcement to the warden, who was grilling him patiently.

"I expect Lyda to show up at any moment." The prisoner twisted his cap in his hands. "I'm surprised she hasn't appeared by this time."

Taken aback, the warden choked on his cigarette smoke. "What did you say?"

"I just said I expect Lyda at any moment."

"My God, man, are you crazy?"

"Not at all. Warden, you don't know Lyda. She's a mighty fine woman. She told me a long time ago that if ever I was grabbed and brought back here, she'd come of her own free will. Give herself up to help me. When she hears you've really brought me back, she'll keep her word."

Thomas stared at the tormented man. "Minton, you seem like an intelligent human being. Do you honestly believe that?"

"Of course. You don't know Lyda."

"I know Lyda. As long as you're willing to take the rap for that woman, you'll rot in this prison."

Minton shook his head. "I don't believe that for a minute, Warden."

"Well, we'll find out. Your capture has made the front page of every paper in the country. Lyda can read. We'll soon know if your theory is correct."

A grim smile creased Minton's face. "She'll come, Warden. She'll come."

Lyda did not appear at the prison gates that day, or the following day, or the next. Finally on the third day, the warden received word that David Minton wanted to see him. The prisoner was duly ushered into the warden's office.

Minton looked terrible. His hands fluttered like a freed canary, his blinking eyes sending tears coursing down his cheeks. "Warden, did Lyda show up?"

"We've seen neither hide nor hair of your girl friend," replied the warden.

"No telephone calls? Nothing?"

"Absolutely nothing."

The prisoner sagged into a chair, his watering eyes grotesquely magnified by his thick glasses. "Okay, Warden. You win."

Thomas stared at his charge. "What do you mean, I win?"

"Simple. You win." The homely man gave vent to a deep sigh. "I do know something about Lyda's whereabouts."

Denver Chief of Police G. T. Clark reread the telegram that had just been handed him. Then he picked up the phone. A short time later Detectives Genty and Turner entered his office.

"Our cashew nut has cracked," said the chief to the two men. "Here's the address of Lyda Southard. 731 Elati Street here in Denver. Get out there and bring that woman back here. Be sure and get her this time. That woman is making an old man out of me."

A police car with Turner at the wheel raced through the late-night streets of Denver. It was nearly midnight when the prowl car pulled up in front of 731 Elati.

The house was dark. The two men mounted the porch. Genty rang the doorbell. No one answered. The lawmen stole quietly around to the back door. They found no signs of any inhabitants. Discouraged, the two men went back to the front door. "I don't want to go back empty-handed," said Genty. "Not again."

"Shall we break in?"

"No. You know the chief takes a dim view of our breaking into houses without a warrant. Let's just wait here on the porch for a spell. This house looks lived in. Maybe its occupant — or occupants — have just gone out for the evening, and will be back."

"Okay." The two men commandeered the front porch swing, lit up smokes, and listened to the swing chain creak as they swung back and forth.

"Did you happen to read the thick file on this woman we're trying to find?"

"Yes," said Turner. "I did my homework."

"I studied it carefully, hoping I might find some kind of pattern that Lyda has established. Some kind of modus operandi."

"Did you find one?"

"Not really. But I thought the role that Deputy Sheriff Virgil Ormsby played in her final apprehension was interesting. That guy deserves a lot of credit."

"That he does. He was a bulldog. It seems that every clue he got turned out to be a place Lyda had just vacated."

"Yep," said Turner, looking over at his partner. "I know just how he feels. We've had our share of flown coops."

"Let's just hope this isn't another one."

Suddenly Turner gripped Genty's arm. "Footsteps. Hear 'em?"

"I hear 'em. Coming this way."

As the sound of footfalls increased, the figure of a man emerged from the darkness. It strode purposefully down the sidewalk and turned in on the walk leading toward the porch occupied by the two men.

Feeling the hair on the nape of his neck beginning to rise, Genty rose to meet the man. "Good evening, sir."

Startled, the man stepped back. "Who are you?"

"We are police officers." Genty flashed his badge. "Detective Turner here, I'm Detective Genty."

The man acknowledged the introduction with a nod. "I'm Harry Whitlock. What can I do for you gentlemen?"

"For starters, you can ask us in."

"Very well." Whitlock unlocked the front door, led the way into the front parlor, snapped on the light. The officers saw a medium-sized man with regular features, in his mid-forties, with wide, brown eyes that were now surveying the two men suspiciously. "Have a seat."

"Thank you, sir." The men sat down.

"Now what's this all about?"

Genty took a deep breath. "This is all rather a painful business, Mr. Whitlock. But first I'll tell you that we must see your wife."

Whitlock looked surprised. "My wife? What has this to do with my wife?"

"We'll explain all that," said Turner. "Now where is she, Mr. Whitlock?"

"She's not here. She left Denver three days ago when she received a long-distance call from her relatives. Her mother is dying in Akron, Ohio. But what has this to do with you? Why do you want to see her?"

Genty shot a swift look at his partner, sighed, and turned to the puzzled Whitlock. "You are probably unaware of this, Mr. Whitlock, but we have reason to believe that your wife is really Lyda Southard. An escaped prisoner from the Idaho State Penitentiary."

The color began to drain from Whitlock's face. "You gentlemen have made a big mistake. You have the wrong woman. My wife's name is Fern Zellars Whitlock."

Turner shook his head. "I'm afraid not, Mr. Whitlock. Her real name is Lyda Southard. And she has murdered five people that we know of. No telling how many more we don't know of."

Whitlock's face became ashen. He tried to speak, but no words would issue.

"I know it's a shock," said Genty, sympathetically, "but you're lucky to know the truth. Lyda's other husbands died without knowing it."

Whitlock raised a protesting hand, searched for his tongue, finally found it. "There must be some mistake. You have the wrong woman. My wife could never do anything like that — "

"No?" said Genty, reaching inside his coat. He pulled out a folded handbill. "Then take a look at this photo. Is this your wife?"

Genty handed Whitlock the police circular with Lyda's picture on it. Whitlock took the paper with shaking hands. He stared at the photo for a moment, then he licked his lips as if to lubricate his voice. "Dear Mother of God!" he said weakly.

"That is your wife, is it not, Mr. Whitlock?" asked Turner.

"Yes. That is my wife." The words were barely audible. "She looks different now. But the resemblance is unmistakable." The police circular slipped from Whitlock's limp hands. As it fluttered to the floor, the befuddled man gazed vacuously at the familiar face staring up at him. His head bowed as he tried to come to grips with this horrible revelation.

Genty reached out a hand to grip the sagging shoulders. "You have our deepest sympathy, Mr. Whitlock. And we know this is tough. But we have to get the answers to a few questions. Will you help us?"

Whitlock straightened up, produced a handkerchief, and blew his nose. After a moment, he looked at the two officers in turn. "I'll help any way I can."

"Thank you, sir," said Genty. "You say your wife left Denver three days ago to hurry to her mother. She is supposed to be sick in Akron, Ohio. Do you have any proof that she actually went to Ohio? Did she leave a forwarding address?"

"No," said Whitlock in a husky whisper. "No forwarding address. All I know is she came down to my place of business several days ago. She was very upset. She said she must leave at once, and she needed money. I drew two weeks' advance on my salary and gave her that. She couldn't even wait for the first train east, so I put her on the eastbound bus. I haven't heard from her since."

"The story of the mother was a fake. Your wife has no mother living in Akron. And, of course, your wife had no intention of going there." Genty stroked his chin, chewing this cud. "This whole thing is beginning to come into focus. When Lyda read in the papers that Minton had been arrested, she thought he wouldn't give her away. She probably figured Minton would stall us, and we'd finally give up and let him go.

"She had the colossal gall to think she still had power over him enough to keep his mouth shut. But when Minton was sent back to Idaho and put back into the Big House, she got scared. She knew the warden would put the screws on him until he cracked. So she decided to skip out."

"Who is Minton?" asked Whitlock, trying to regain control of himself. "I never heard of him."

Genty took another police circular from his coat pocket. He handed the flyer containing Minton's picture to the husband.

Whitlock swore. "Good God, that's Dave Rains. My wife's half-brother. He came to the house often."

"Half-brother, eh?" Genty gave vent to a tired smile. "He's no relation to your wife. The name Rains is an alias. He helped Lyda escape from prison. They were passing as husband and wife before she married you. This afternoon he confessed everything over at the Idaho State Pen. Told the warden how she had married you, and gave him this address."

Turner looked over at the man who was gazing at the floor with numb eyes. "Now do you believe your wife is not who she claims she is?"

"I guess so. I don't know. I'm so confused."

"We understand that, Mr. Whitlock," said Genty. "But there's one way we have a good chance of catching her. It may or may not work. But we need your cooperation. Can we count on you?"

Whitlock blew his nose again, wiped it. "I guess so."

"Good. Here's the plan. The way I see it, Lyda didn't reach Ohio. Probably didn't want to spend all her money. She more than likely hopped to a nearby state, where she's now hiding in some town. She'll do one of two things: she'll find a job, support herself, and you'll never hear of her again. Or she'll write to you for more money.

"Since we're in a depression, she may find it hard to get a job. But she'll never write to you if the news leaks out that Minton has confessed, or if she knows we've learned about her life with you. So we've got to keep a lid on the fact that Minton blabbed. If that hits the papers, which I understand she reads religiously, we're dead ducks. Am I getting through to you, Mr. Whitlock?"

"I understand."

"Good. To repeat, don't say a word to anyone about this. Not even to your relatives and best friends. Play dumb, act as if you knew nothing about your wife's true identity. That you expect to hear from her any day. Then if she writes you, we'll pounce on it."

Whitlock nodded, still in a daze. From his expression, the two detectives divined that his mind was flashing back to the moments he had shared with his wife. He had been intimate with a woman who had been convicted of murdering at least four husbands, and was now wanted in half a dozen states. During the questioning, a pained look had crossed his face, suggesting some extraordinary recollection.

Turner took up the questioning. "Would you mind telling us how you happened to meet Lyda? And how she ended up in your bed?"

Whitlock smiled ruefully. "I'll tell you everything. My first wife died last year. In the latter part of last December, I advertised in the Denver newspapers for a housekeeper. My mother was bedridden, and I have an eight-year-old son. I needed someone to look after them.

"Fern — or this woman you call Lyda Southard — answered the ad. She said her name was Fern Zellars Rains. She claimed to be a good cook and had worked as a practical nurse. I hired her immediately." He paused, as if to quell some memory that had surfaced, then continued. "I liked her from the first. She was an excellent cook, and she also took very good care of my mother and my little boy. She was very pleasant to be with. She only had one small flaw."

"And what was that?" asked Turner, sitting on the edge of his chair.

"She was a bit of a prude. And she had some overstrict religious ideas. Even before my mother died, Fern used to say it wasn't quite right for her to be living in the same house with me. Also, she was very strict with Buddy, my son. She taught him hymns, and they used to sing them every night after dinner. Occasionally this man you call Minton visited her. As I told you, she introduced him to me as her half-brother.

"Well, things went along pretty well until February of this year. That's when my mother died. Shortly after that Fern confided in me that her half-brother objected to her staying on as my housekeeper. She explained that Dave said it would sully her reputation. I saw her point. She had such a strict regard for appearances that it bothered her.

"I had this feeling she was trying to pressure me into marrying her. I gave it a lot of thought, then decided it was important to have someone make a good home for my boy. So I proposed marriage. She readily accepted, and I set a June date. But she came to me the next day and said her brother objected to a date so far in the future. She went on to explain that we'd been living in the same house in an unmarried state for several months, and the neighbors were beginning to talk."

A smile flirted with Genty's lips. "That's our girl Lyda. She has a funny idea about protecting one's reputation."

Whitlock gave another rueful smile. "I capitulated. We were married in March." Then his face suddenly brightened. "In the light of what you have just told me, this will explain an odd happening."

"What is that?" asked Turner.

"Well, I have some friends on the police force. On the night after the wedding we were having a little party here to celebrate. Suddenly the door opened, and several of my cop friends came in, wearing their uniforms. When my wife looked up to see all those policeman, she tottered against the mantelpiece. I rushed over, asked her what was the matter. When she saw the cops were only making a social call, she seemed to relax. She said the room was warm, and she suddenly felt faint." Whitlock's eyes swept the faces of the two lawmen. "Now I understand why she almost fainted."

Genty nodded. "Cops in uniform do seem to make an impression. Especially on criminals. Go on, Mr. Whitlock."

"Well, our life went as smoothly as could be expected. There was only one thing that seriously disturbed me about Fern. She kept a small bottle of poison in her bureau drawer. Every time she left the house she would slip it into her purse. Naturally concerned, I asked her about the poison. She said she had had such a tragic early life that if anything else terrible happened to her she would drink the poison. I tried to find out what great tragedy had befallen her, but she wouldn't say." Whitlock groaned.

"That is not the world's greatest foundation for a happy married life," said Turner.

"Did she take the bottle of poison when she left home?" asked Genty.

"Yes. When I returned home from seeing her off on the bus, I checked. The poison was gone."

Turner addressed Genty. "That compounds our problem. It means she won't be taken alive if she can help it."

Genty nodded in agreement. "Mr. Whitlock, have you any reason to believe that any member of your family has ever been poisoned?"

Whitlock turned troubled eyes on the detective. "Not that I know of."

"How about your mother?"

"Well, she was an old lady. And she had been sick for some time before Fern came to the house. The doctor said she had died of old age and a combination of diseases."

"But she did die not long after Lyda moved into your house?"

Whitlock's eyes bugged. "Why, yes, come to think of it."

"Could be coincidence," said Genty, hoping to calm the dumbstruck man rooted to the edge of his chair. "Did Lyda ever suggest that you take out insurance?"

Whitlock thought for a moment. "Yes. Yes, she did. I recall that she began urging me to buy insurance shortly after we were married. She suggested a twenty-thousand-dollar policy. I postponed taking it out, however."

Genty slapped his knee. "That's it! She was working on you to get a policy, just like she worked her other husbands. It was lucky you didn't buy that insurance. You might be worm-bait six feet under the ground by this time."

"Oh, Jesus!" Whitlock shuddered. "How did she kill her other husbands?"

"With arsenic," Genty answered. "Arsenic boiled out of black flypaper. By the way, did she bring any of that kind of flypaper into your house?"

Whitlock shook his head. "I never saw any. But now that you mention poison, I do remember something else. About a month ago, my boy, Buddy, was taken sick. We couldn't tell what was the matter with him. I thought it was something he might have eaten that didn't agree with him. He would get better for a few days, then suddenly take a turn for the worse. Fern was nursing him all the time."

"Did you call a doctor?" asked Turner.

"I wanted to right away. But Fern insisted it wasn't necessary, that she would nurse him back to health. But I finally did call the doctor. He diagnosed it as acute indigestion. Then, early in July, my wife came to me and said I needn't worry about Buddy, that she was sure she could pull him through. She started feeding him whites of eggs, and he started getting better right away. It was miraculous. In a few days he was up and around, acting normally."

The two detectives had hung on every word of Whitlock's statement. Suddenly Genty turned to Turner, his eyes afire with excitement. "Do you see how this all adds up?" He turned back to Whitlock. "Can you recall the precise date when your wife said the boy would pull through, and began feeding him whites of eggs?"

Whitlock shot his inquisitor a puzzled look. "Why, yes. I remember it well. It was the second of July."

"That's right!" Genty slapped the palm of his hand with his fist. "On July second your wife got word that Minton had been arrested. She was scared. What if Minton blew the whistle on her? Rather than add yet another crime to her lurid past, she decided to let up on the boy. The whites of eggs are an antidote for poison. She knew it."

Whitlock could only stare at the detective, beads of perspiration covering his forehead.

"You paint one hell of a picture of a narrowly averted tragedy," said Genty. "In my opinion, the capture of Minton saved your son's life, and yours as well. I hope you'll work with us to bring that woman back where she can be put away and prevented from doing any more harm. I know what a blow this is, Mr. Whitlock. But your wife's a natural killer. We'll need your help to make sure she doesn't find any more victims."

The two detectives stood up, Whitlock mounting shaking legs to do likewise. Unsteadily, he accompanied them to the front door. He shook hands with each of the men. "You can depend on me." The words came out as a whisper.

"And take care of yourself, Mr. Whitlock," said Turner. "Do you want us to send a doctor over with a sedative?"

"No. Thank you. I'll be fine."

"You sure? You're shaking like a hound dog trying to pass peach pits."

"Well, gentlemen, there is something else you should know. I'll tell you now, you'll find it out anyway."

"Shoot," said Turner.

"This will sound crazy. But my first wife, Hazel, committed suicide on August the fifteenth. Four months before Lyda answered my ad in the newspaper."

"That so?" asked Genty. "How did your wife die?"

Whitlock took a deep breath. "Poison."

Genty looked at Turner. "Poison?"

"Yes. Hazel and I had an argument in the kitchen. We didn't get along very well. The argument got violent. All of a sudden I saw Hazel grab some poison tablets, and before I could wrestle them away from her, she had swallowed them. I rushed her to Denver General Hospital. She died there."

"My God!" muttered Turner.

"I was taken to police headquarters for questioning, but charges were never filed." Whitlock swabbed his forehead with his handkerchief. "So you can see why I'm a bit touchy about poison."

Turner grunted. "We'll check out your story at headquarters."

"Please do that. After my wife's death, I brought my aged mother home to live with me. She was not well, which is another reason I hired this woman you call Lyda. She said she was a graduate nurse from the Mayo Clinic in Rochester, Minnesota. And she would also take good care of my boy."

"In a way, you're a very lucky man, Mr. Whitlock."

"Yeah. I'm some lucky guy."

"Well, take it easy. We'll be in touch."

"Thank you, gentlemen. For your consideration."

"Don't mention it."

Whitlock saw the men to the door, and as they exited he said, "Just one more thing, gentlemen. I have a favor to ask."

"A favor?" asked Genty.

"Yes, sir. Since I have agreed to keep Lyda's identity a secret, would you be kind enough to let me publish a legal notice in the *Denver Post* that I am no longer responsible for my wife's debts?"

As the two detectives walked down the street toward the prowl car, Genty turned to Turner. "This case is getting screwier by the minute. What do you make of Whitlock?"

"I know he's more nervous than a long-tailed pussycat in a room full of rocking chairs. But then, who wouldn't be?"

"Think he's telling the truth?"

"Probably."

Genty got into the car, fumbling for his keys. He turned to his partner. "You know what I like about this job?"

"No," said Turner, crawling into the front seat. "What do you like about this job?"

"It's such a pleasant line of work. We just spent a delightful night telling a nice guy that he's been sleeping with a notorious murderer. That poor soul won't go to bed for a week."

"Yep," agreed Turner. "According to the files, this is the second husband the cops had to tell that his new bride had poisoned a passel of husbands."

"Yeah. Guy by the name of Paul Southard. Navy man." Genty turned on the ignition. "Yes, sir. We picked a great profession." He turned to his partner. "Next life let's look into being used-car salesmen."

Genty grunted. "Always wanted to be a bartender myself."

Chapter Seventeen

The days passed on a plodding treadmill. The police worked hard but got nowhere. Information concerning Lyda Southard's latest getaway was sent secretly to police chiefs throughout the nation.

An attempt was made to trace her on the eastbound stage out of Denver, but to no avail. Priority bulletins were sent to neighboring states: Kansas, Nebraska, Wyoming, Utah, Arizona, New Mexico, and Oklahoma. No word of David Minton's confession had been allowed to leak to the press; to all outward appearances the search for the female fugitive had been abandoned.

Still no letter came to the home of Harry Whitlock from his missing wife. Meanwhile, the police had brought in Minton's sister for questioning. Under a grilling by Chief of Police Clark, she admitted she had tipped off Lyda at Minton's suggestion right after his arrest. She also confessed that she had notified Lyda as soon as she learned her brother was leaving for the Idaho penitentiary with Warden Thomas.

But a thorough questioning of the homely woman convinced the lawmen she did not know where Lyda Whitlock had gone when she had fled from Denver.

Denver District Attorney Earl Wettengel investigated the death of Theodosia Whitlock, Lyda's mother-in-law, but could find no evidence of foul play that might require a postmortem. The Whitlock house was searched, but no traces of black flypaper or arsenic were found. If Lyda had tried to poison young Buddy Whitlock, she had learned from previous experiences and had destroyed the evidence.

Two weeks passed. The Denver police and Warden Thomas in

Idaho marked the days off the calendar, hoping against hope that the crafty fugitive would show her hand. They had no desire to apprehend her by tracking down a trail of poisoned carcasses.

July 29. Chief Clark received a phone call at his office. He could barely make out the words of a very excited Harry Whitlock. "I have some news. Would you send Detectives Turner and Genty out to my house right away?"

The two sleuths lost no time in finding themselves in the parlor where they had first listened to Whitlock's recital. Hands shaking, Whitlock reached into his pocket. He produced an envelope. "Here it is," he said. "A letter from my wife. Just came today. It's postmarked Topeka, Kansas. July twenty-seventh."

Genty and Turner read the letter in silence. It said that Whitlock's wife and her mother were in Topeka visiting relatives. Her mother had improved greatly. She would be returning home in about two weeks. She asked Whitlock to send her some money in care of General Delivery at Topeka.

Genty handed the letter back to Whitlock. "It's going to work! By God, we'll nail her this time. She thinks Minton hasn't confessed and that she's safe. She doesn't know we know anything about you. Now here's what you do. You write her in care of General Delivery in Topeka, just like she says. We'll wire the Topeka police. Have them pick her up when she goes to the General Delivery window to pick up her mail."

A medley of emotions played on Whitlock's face as he stared at the two men. Then in a soft voice he said, "I'll get a letter off to her tonight."

Perry Brush was the chief of police for Topeka, Kansas. A powerful, heavy-set man with white hair, he pushed the glasses up on his nose and addressed the two men sitting in front of him. "You know about Lyda Southard, the gal who's allergic to live husbands?"

Captain Morris Leonard and Detective Victor Plants nodded.

"We've just got the word that she's visiting our fair city. I want every cop to study her photo and be on the lookout for her. Now here's our lead. Her most recent husband is a Denver man named Harry Whitlock. She's probably going by the name of Mrs. Harry Whitlock, or Fern Zellars Rains, her previous alias.

"She's written to Whitlock asking him to send her money here. Care of General Delivery. Now you gents contact the postal authorities. I want someone to watch that General Delivery window every moment it's open. When she asks for the letter, grab her. Got that?"

Again the two men nodded, jotting in their notebooks.

"Also, I want you to have your men watch for her on the streets, at the railroad station, at all depots for departing auto stages. And one other thing you men will have to be alert for. She's liable to try suicide. She may have a gun, or more likely, she may have a bottle of poison. So be careful. We're dealing with a very dangerous and desperate woman."

Captain Leonard and Detective Plants distributed police circulars containing Lyda's photo to all the men on the Topeka police force. Then a citywide search was conducted. Next morning, on July 30, when the General Delivery window was opened, a detective was there watchfully waiting. It was a little early for Lyda to expect a letter from her husband, but the police were taking no chances in case she appeared.

The hours dragged by. Several false alarms snapped the detective out of his boredom, but no one inquired for letters addressed to Mrs. Harry Whitlock or Fern Zellars Rains. The General Delivery window closed, the detective went back to the precinct empty-handed. Nor did the cops stationed throughout the city catch sight of the escapee.

The next day was hot and sunny, a typical Kansas summer day. Detective Victor Plants reported to the Topeka post office ten minutes before the General Delivery window was to open. A tall man, wearing a light worsted gray suit and a soft-brimmed straw hat, Plants slouched in a corner of the post office, obviously absorbed in a new best-selling novel by Pearl S. Buck called *The Good Earth*. One would be hard-pressed to recognize the man as a gimlet-eyed policeman watching every movement in the post office.

The morning hours ticked by slowly. Detective Plants peered out from under the brim of his straw hat and sized up several women who had approached the General Delivery window. There had been no sign from the postal clerk. He went back to ostensibly burying himself in his book.

It was nearly eleven o'clock. A stocky, pleasant-faced woman entered the front door. Wearing a lavender print dress with a matching straw hat, the woman seemed to be looking furtively around her as she strode to the General Delivery window. Detective Plants glanced up at her, touched the brim of his hat, and went back to his book.

The woman smiled at him. She had dark hair, sharp blue eyes that were nearly obscured by spectacles with dark brown rims. She had a jutting chin, her neck was thick, she had wide shoulders and hips. As she came to the window she tucked her large purse up under her left arm.

"Do you have a letter for Mrs. Harry Whitlock?" came the low-voiced query.

"Mrs. Harry Whitlock, you say?" verified the clerk on the other side of the window.

"Yes."

The clerk looked over at the man slouching over one of the writing tables, and pushed his visor up with his thumb. Then he started shuffling through a handful of letters. "Ah, here we are. Mrs. Harry Whitlock." He handed the letter to the woman. She took it, thanked him, and walked over to one of the high writing desks.

She put her purse down on the desk and started to tear open the letter. Then she suddenly stopped. Out of the corner of her eye she saw a large hand come down on the purse. She felt another hand on her arm. She spun around, looked up into Detective Plant's face.

"You're Lyda Southard Whitlock," Plants said in a low voice. "I'm from police headquarters."

The woman stood perfectly still, as her body turned to stone. Then suddenly, her knees buckled. Plant put his arms around her waist, holding her up. Her eyes started to close in a faint, then suddenly her body gave a spasmodic jerk. She slowly opened her eyes, fixing them on the detective as she began to regain control of her faculties. She straightened up, rearranged her hat, and gave him a tired smile. "I've been expecting you."

"And we've been looking for you, Mrs. Whitlock. Would you come with me, please?"

"All right." Her voice was low, almost gravelly. "I'll come quietly if you won't use those terrible handcuffs."

"That's fair."

"Before we go, may I have my purse, please? I seem to have mussed up my hair."

"You look just fine. Your purse will be returned at the police station."

"Very well." She gave the detective a half-smile, tilted her head up and took his arm. "Shall we go?"

Topeka Chief of Police Perry Brush rose as Detective Plants entered his office with Lyda Whitlock on his arm. Almost gallantly, the detective ushered her over to a chair and held it for her as she sat down.

"So you are Mrs. Lyda Southard," said the chief, eyeing her curiously.

"Mrs. Lyda Whitlock," corrected the prisoner.

"Of course. I'm Police Chief Perry Brush."

"Glad to make your acquaintance, Chief Brush." She smiled at him, then turned to Plants. "I wonder if I might have my purse now, Detective? My hair must be a mess."

"One moment." Plants opened her purse, searched through it for a moment, then removed a small, black bottle. "I don't think you'll be needing this." He handed her the purse.

She took the purse, pulled out a compact, checked her face in its mirror. Then she snapped it shut, replaced it in the purse. "You know, gentlemen, there's something I have to confess."

"Oh?" said the chief. "What would that be, Mrs. Whitlock?"

She suddenly sagged, turned tired eyes on the two men. "I must confess I'm glad it's over."

The following morning the neighbors of Harry Whitlock received the shock of their lives as they read the headlines in their morning paper.

That sweet-faced little homebody, Mrs. Fern Whitlock, with whom they had gossiped, shared gardening chores, and exchanged recipes, had been arrested and branded as an escaped murderess. It just couldn't be. The neighbors remembered Fern's — or Lyda's — friendly smile, her infectious sense of humor. The latter, however, often being at odds with her expressions of religious matters, which were delivered in a fervent and strident manner.

And when the neighbors recalled the meals they had shared at the home of a famous poisoner, their spines shuddered with cold chills. They would never, ever forget their next-door neighbor, Mrs. Lyda Trueblood-Dooley-McHaffie-Lewis-Meyer-Southard-Whitlock.

Her first night in the Topeka jail, Lyda wept almost constantly, as if a large, pent-up dam had broken.

Warden and Mrs. Thomas arrived from Boise to pick up their long-time fugitive and return her to prison. Lyda gave the Thomases a friendly greeting as they checked in at the Topeka jail. She grabbed both of Mrs. Thomas's hands. "Hello. I'm glad to see you again."

"Hello, Lyda," said Mrs. Thomas.

She apologized for escaping. "You'll have no more trouble with me from now on."

Lyda told the warden she would waive extradition. Thomas replied that their train back to Boise would leave that night at 6:50.

Although the warden's wife shared a sleeping compartment with Lyda on the westbound train, the warden took no chances. He took up sentry duty in a chair outside of her chambers all night. "She might try something," he explained to the porter. "She slipped through my fingers once, but it won't happen again. I won't breathe easy until she's back in her cell."

At a brief stopover in Denver, Detective Henry Genty and several newsmen from the *Rocky Mountain News* and the *Denver Post* were waiting at the station. They boarded Union Pacific No. 21, filed through the train until they came across Warden Thomas having a smoke in the vestibule. Genty introduced himself, telling Thomas he wanted to ask Lyda how she had eluded him in Denver. And he wanted to see what kind of a woman Lyda really was.

"She's in a very bad humor this morning," said Thomas. "I tried to get her to take a walk, but she refused."

"May we go in for just a minute, Warden?" asked Genty. "Our Denver press would like to ask her a few questions."

Feeling obligated to a fellow lawman, especially one who had spent a considerable time trying to track down his fugitive, the warden acquiesced. "But please make it brief, gentlemen. We're scheduled to pull out shortly."

Agreeing, the men crowded into the small train compartment. Lyda was sitting in the corner wearing a blue print dress. Her hair was dyed black and she looked older than her thirty-nine years. She looked out the window and refused to talk. She covered her face with a napkin.

The reporters shot questions at her: "Do you deny poisoning Harry Whitlock's mother? Did you poison Whitlock's nine-year-old son, Benny? District Attorney Earl Wettengel has launched an investigation to determine whether Theodosia Whitlock had been poisoned. What's your response, Lyda?"

Lyda merely shrugged, seeking refuge behind the napkin pressed to her face.

While flashbulbs popped, the warden finally succeeded in ushering the press out of the compartment. As he left, Detective Genty thanked the warden and shook his hand. "I must admit," said the detective, "that Lyda is not what I had imagined."

Thomas grinned. "People have a tendency to over-glamorize a notorious figure."

"I suppose. Frankly, she looks just like a dumpy little housekeeper. I'll be damned if I can see how she attracted all these men."

"Well, she's got something. Even at her age. She has the Pullman porter eating out of her hand." Thomas shook his head. "She certainly has some kind of sexual magnetism."

"Yeah, I guess. I just wish we could bottle it. We could make a fortune."

"Amen to that."

On the last leg of their train ride home, Warden Thomas was jubilant. His job was now on a much more secure footing. At last he would be able to mute the critics in the press who had long maintained that the elusive Lyda was far too clever to ever be apprehended by the police.

Their plumpish ward, however, did not seem to share the warden's euphoria. Lyda had developed a laconic demeanor as the clacking train wheels moved her ever closer to the walls of her old home. She was quiet, somber; a woman whose emotions had been completely spent. The long months of strain and fear in eluding capture had taken a tremendous toll on her nervous energy.

But as the train approached Boise early on the morning of August 4 (exactly fifteen months since her escape), a transformation came over the prisoner. Already famous, she knew that she would again be in the spotlight. She rose before sunrise, donned her best finery: a light-blue dress, close-fitting turban, fawn-colored shoes, and silk hose. Every strand of her hair was in place, her face powdered, her lips rouged.

No sooner had the train jarred to a stop in the Boise station than she appeared in the doorway of her Pullman, flashing a bright smile at several hundred of the press and the curious who crowded the station platform. She waved, shouting "Hello, everybody!"

Then, like a movie queen, she swept down the train steps and, accompanied by Warden and Mrs. Thomas, stepped toward the prison car. In sharp contrast to Lyda's jaunty manner, Warden Thomas's wife showed deep lines of fatigue from having to keep close watch on her charge during the train trip. The good woman missed the bottom stair of the car and would have fallen to grievous damage had it not been for the alert assistance of the train conductor.

At the prison that afternoon Lyda held informal levee. She posed for cameramen and answered reporters' questions with smiling patience. She obviously reveled in the limelight, undoubtedly aware that it would probably be her last personal appearance for years to come.

She recounted the details of her escape, displaying two rusty saws that she had used to cut the bar in her cell. They had remained buried in the yard of the women's quarters until Lyda had returned to show the guards their location. "I was a fool," she said, "for ever having left." She divulged how she had arranged with Minton to escape several weeks before her disappearance. Minton had tossed notes over the wall to keep her apprised of developments.

When pressed by the reporters, Lyda disclosed two interesting revelations: her alleged fondness for Whitlock and his family, and her disdain for David Minton. In spite of the fact that Minton had stood staunchly by her up to a certain point, the hapless man was a victim of haranguing vituperation. It was Minton, declared Lyda, who had persuaded her to escape; she hadn't really wanted to leave her rose gardens. She had always suspected that Minton might double-cross her, and indeed he had.

Her latest husband, Harry Whitlock, however, was cut from a different bolt. "He was an educated man," as Lyda put it. "He had personality and he played the harp-guitar beautifully . . . he was very good to me . . . he has a wonderful little boy . . . there was nothing to the statement that I had anything to do with the boy's illness . . . or with the death of Mr. Whitlock's mother . . . the statement that I asked Mr. Whitlock to take out insurance was an absolute falsehood."

Lyda was gay, almost sparkling, throughout the interview. Especially when recounting the fact that she — a supposedly notorious outlaw — had gone to a dance in Fort Collins, Colorado, and had danced with more than one police officer. She delighted in pandering to the prurience of the journalists present, many of whom were less than circumspect in their coverage of the lurid details surrounding this complex woman.

And then her moment in the sun drew to a close. The reporters and the cameramen packed up their gear, climbed into their cars, and drove back to Boise. Lyda was taken in tow by Mrs. Thomas and a prison matron. The summer sun sank slowly behind the Idaho hills while holding hands with the morale of Lyda Whitlock.

While being photographed in the prison gallery, several changes were noticed in the face of the plumpish prisoner. Lyda's red hair had been dyed black, and two front teeth had been replaced with gold. Then she was led across the roadway to the wall surrounding the women's quarters. A new heavy iron door was unlocked. Lyda went inside and walked briskly across the enclosure to the little square prison house she knew so well.

She was ushered inside to her old cell, which now held strong new bars in the window. She looked up through the tiny square window at the little patch of blue sky. Then she slowly sank down on her cot, clapped her hands over her face, and broke into wracking, sobbing tears.

"Jesus Christ!" Warden Thomas slammed his fist down on the letter on his desk. "I don't believe this!"

The head turnkey, startled by the noise from the warden's office, poked his head in the door. "Something wrong, Warden?"

"Wrong! Sam, read this." Thomas waved the letter at the jailer.

The jailer entered the warden's office, took the letter from his perturbed boss. He read:

Dear Warden Thomas:

I don't write too good, but being of sound mind and body, I want to make the following confession that follows:

Lyda Southard is innocent of all the crimes she has been accused of. Lyda could not possibly poison no one. I am the one that put arsenic in the food of all her husbands. I have always loved Lyda, and when I could not have her I could not stand to see other men have her. So I poisoned them with rat poison.

Now that you know who done it, I know you will want to see justus done, and will release Lyda from her jail cell. Because she is innocent.

Yours truley,

David Minton

"My God!" said the jailer, his eyes popping. "What do you make of this, Warden?"

Thomas shook his head. "We'll have to check it out." His eyes focused on the inkwell that had spilled when he slammed his fist down on his desk. "But I will say this. This Minton character sure has a hard-on for our Miss Lyda."

"That's for sure." The jailer took out his bandana and mopped the spilled ink from his boss's desk. "Wouldn't that be a kick in the head if Lyda was innocent after all this?"

The warden turned his eyes on his turnkey. "My God, man, don't even think of it!"

The investigation of David Minton's confession letter did not take long. When pressed for dates and facts of his alleged poisonings, Minton replied with complete gibberish. And the fact that he had been serving time in jail during the period in which he claimed to have poisoned one of Lyda's husbands did little to bolster his credibility.

A week later, David C. Minton, commonly known as "Gaspipe," was hailed before Judge Charles E. Winstead in Boise. Minton confessed to writing the phony confession, and he pleaded guilty to the crime of assisting a prisoner to escape. On August 6, 1932, Minton was sentenced to from one to five years in the Idaho penitentiary.

Meanwhile, in Denver, a very shaken Harry Whitlock started a court action to annul his marriage to Lyda.

Shortly after Lyda's reincarceration, Warden Thomas was being interviewed by a reporter from the *Boise Capital News.* "Warden," asked the newsman, "do you have any explanation for Lyda Southard's strange crimes, and her insatiable appetite for murder?"

Thomas swiveled around in his chair to face the reporter. "The best I can determine from talking to psychologists, Mike, is that Lyda is what they call emotionally deficient. In other words, while Lyda appears perfectly normal, she does not respond to certain things as do normal people.

She has no feelings, hence no sense of responsibility."

"How can this be?" asked the reporter, looking up from his notes.

"Well, it's true to a certain extent of many murderers. But Lyda is an extreme example. I recently talked to a famous psychiatrist in Chicago, Dr. Orlando F. Scott. He has a great reputation for knowing the criminal mind. He says that every human being has two minds. Two brains. The lower brain, or basal ganglia, controls the emotions. In Lyda's case, the lower brain is out of whack."

"Afraid you're losing me, Warden."

"I don't go much for psychiatric mumbo-jumbo myself. Sometimes I think the head-shrinkers should be the ones in the padded rooms. But it's interesting that so many other celebrated women killers have selected the same method as Lyda — poison by arsenic."

"You mean our local celebrity is not the only one who has resorted to the hemlock cup?"

"By no means." Thomas leaned back in his chair, staring at the ceiling as he dredged his memory. "There is the celebrated case of Bertha Gifford of Catawissa, Missouri. In 1928 she was charged with poisoning a neighbor she was not overly fond of. Investigators unearthed sixteen other victims she was charged with tucking away. The jury found her not guilty for reasons of insanity.

"Interesting," said the reporter, scribbling furiously.

"And there was the notorious French nurse named Antoinette Scierri. She poisoned her fiance, and when the gendarmes investigated, they uncovered twelve other murders which they attributed to Antoinette. Antoinette lost her head for the last time on the French guillotine."

"This is great stuff, Warden."

"It gets better. All of this pales compared to the famous case of the Hungarian women prisoners of the villages of Nagyrev and Tizakurt. These lively ladies, led by a domineering old hag named Susi Olah, were held responsible for more than a hundred murders by arsenical poisoning. Susi and some of her women lieutenants committed suicide, two women were hanged, others were sent to prison. This all happened only a couple years ago."

"Shit, Warden, I never realized women were so handy with arsenic bottles. I'm gonna rush right home and check my medicine closet."

Thomas grinned. "I think women like poison because it's not so messy. Guns, knives, hatchets . . . they can really make a bloody mess. Since the women have to keep the house clean, it makes sense to be tidy when dispatching one's foes."

"I never looked at it quite that way," said the reporter. "Then our Lyda was not the first one to dispatch her enemies with arsenic."

"By no means. But I'll wager there was no one more ruthless, daring, and cunning than our own Lady Bluebeard. In fact, we've coined a new term for her modus operandi."

"And what is that, sir?"

"Lyda was effective in producing a series of events. She sort of went from one episode to another. Just like the serials in the *Saturday Evening Post*. So we have named her the Serial Killer."

"Serial killer." The reporter moistened his pencil with the tip of his tongue. "Serial killer. That's kind of catchy. Will make a great headline."

"It does seem to fit her. She may be the first to be called that, but I doubt very much if she'll be the last."

The reporter rose, stuffed his notebook into his coat pocket. "If I'm any judge of human nature, you're probably right."

In spite of her heaviness, Lyda was still an attractive woman, and very popular with the other inmates. The women prisoners threw a welcoming party for her return, and she soon fell into her old routine. She was allowed to plant flowers, but there were no trellises for her roses.

She was kept under strict surveillance, the warden having no desire to have his reputation impugned again by this portly woman. In the men's quarters, across the road from Lyda, a gray-haired, myopic convict paced the yard. Occasionally he stopped, glanced in the direction of the women's ward.

One can only imagine what David "Gaspipe" Minton was thinking, as his mouth silently formed words that were never uttered.

Chapter Eighteen

For the next decade the metronome of time ticked its slow, relentless cadence. President Roosevelt was reelected by a landslide, Chiang Kai-shek declared war against Japan, Hilter started his march across Europe, and preparations began for World War II.

Greta Garbo was better known than Adolf Hitler, Picasso painted a mural for the Paris World Exhibition, John Steinbeck won a Pulitzer Prize for a novel call *The Grapes of Wrath*, and a movie called *Gone With the Wind* won an Academy Award and censorship form the Catholic League of Decency for using the word "damn."

But the storm clouds brewing around the world have little or no effect on the inmates of a prison. As if the gray walls provided insulation from the churning chaos of the outside world, the prisoners of the Idaho State Penitentiary went about their monotonous grind as usual, day after day, week after week, year after year.

In 1933 George F. Rudd replaced R. E. Thomas as warden of the Idaho State Penitentiary. Prison reform was in the wind, and it was exemplified by a report from the new warden's Activities and Work Program: "Increased athletic and recreational activities will do a great deal towards keeping up the morale and physical well being of the inmate and his body. Games such as handball, baseball, volley-ball, etc., are to be encouraged ... it is necessary to keep active the mental and physical process of the prisoner. Without diversion the bodies and minds of incarcerated men and women will rapidly deteriorate. The advent of the motion-picture and like entertainment in penitentiary life is not an attempt on the part of the responsible authorities to coddle prisoners or to follow the line of least

172

resistance but rather, to establish breaks in morbid thought chains and disrupt fixations."

In line with this new concept, the prison fostered its own baseball team called the Outlaws. They soon became one of the best teams in Idaho, as attested to by a young baseball player named Floyd Eshelman. "On July 4, 1935," reported the young pitcher, "I played baseball against the Outlaws of the Idaho State Penitentiary. They was the best team I ever played against. I was seventeen years old and pitched for the Ustick Community Team. We thought we were pretty good. We arrived and took our positions along the first base line and the Outlaw team occupied the 3rd base to home position. One of our coaches was allowed in the third base coaching box. No one else was allowed on that side between home and third.

"The field was marked off and a line was drawn on the wall. A home run was right over the guard house on the wall, a small area. The Outlaw team all had alias names. The catchers name was Blanket. There was Billy the Kid and other famous outlaw names. An Outlaw player had to get permission from a guard on the wall before he could enter an area near the wall, but he would signal the guard and practically climb the wall to catch a fly ball. The Outlaws were a most friendly team. Those guys was better than the Pilot team of Boise. In the seventh and eighth innings I was called in to pitch. I was a kid and got the full support of the whole prison rooting section. I had a very good curve ball. I fanned the first batter, the crowd gave me a loud ovation. I could get two strikes but couldn't get the third. In two innings I fanned two. I was glad when the game was over. Even though we were beat badly it was a highlight in my life."

During this period Lyda toiled in her garden; she sewed for herself and some of the other women inmates. Thanks to special permission from the warden, she was allowed to visit a few male inmates, particularly dynamiter Harry Orchard, of whom she was especially fond. Orchard's case was later to become even more of a *cause célèbre* when he was finally granted parole from prison. The new prison reform program had obviously had a very salutory effect on the assassin, for when his parole date arrived, Orchard refused to vacate his cell.

To the astonishment of prison officials, he steadfastly maintained that the penitentiary was the only real home he had ever known, and that he was too old to be thrust out into the cold cruel world. He pleaded for his parole to be turned down. The authorities, conditioned more to preventing prison breakouts than delivering eviction notices, were at a loss as to how to handle a situation in which a prisoner begged to spend the rest of his life in his jail cell.

Things were at a definite impasse until an agreement was finally reached between Orchard and the prison authorities. The dynamiter would be moved out of the prison and across the road, where he would be allowed to build a small shack. Here he would live while raising poultry for the prison inmates. This way he would no longer be sucking from the public trough at taxpayer's expense, yet he still would be near the compound of the penitentiary that he loved so well.

Thus, one of the country's most notorious murderers finally found contentment in running a turkey farm across the street from the prison. The likable assassin became such a part of the institution that in later years, when his health began to deteriorate, he was allowed back into the prison infirmary, and his last wish was fulfilled — to die in the Idaho State Penitentiary.

Another contemporary of Lyda's also proved a sore vexation to prison authorities. A cop-killer with the surname of Van Vlack presented an even knottier problem to the officials than had Orchard. It seems that Van Vlack had been sentenced to hang for shooting several people. On the eve of his execution, his mother paid a last visit to her son, and as she left the cell, he managed to slip out. Before he could be detained, he had leaped to the ceiling rafters, from which he proclaimed, "I am not going to be the entertainment for a bunch of ghoulish onlookers!"

This said, he executed a swan dive, ricocheting off a wall radiator before plunging to the cement floor some three stories below. Van Vlack was grievously injured, but not dead. Once again the horns of a demon dilemma plagued the prison officials. Van Vlack was scheduled to hang in the early morning hours, but he was hardly in any condition to mount the gallows. Should the execution proceed as planned, or would it be more humane to try and make the convict well again, so they could then hang him?

This debate, which eventually involved the governor, would undoubtedly be raging to this day had the condemned man not had the foresight to pass away shortly before the time scheduled for his execution. Although this timely demise neatly took the Idaho prison officials off the hook, what if the inmate had not died? Should the execution have proceeded as planned? This ethical question may well be jawboned by law students for years to come.

In 1933, the possibility of Lyda's parole began to be considered by prison authorities. Lest there be any chance of this happening, that year, according to prison records, several people in Twin Falls wrote letters to the Board of Pardons asking them to deny any request for Lyda's parole. Marcus J. Ware's was one of them:

"Southard began going with a young man living a short distance from my home," he wrote. "This young man had served with the Lost Battalion in France, had been gassed several times, his condition of health was bad on account of this gas, and he had a policy of insurance with the federal government—all of which contributed to Lyda Southard's manifestation of attention to him. There is no doubt in my mind that had he married this woman, he would be a dead man."

In a prison interview on April 13, 1935, Associated Press writer Walter B. Botcher reported that Lyda again denied any guilt in killing her husbands:

"The verdict was unjust," she said. "I still remember my lawyer's last words to the jury: 'She has eternal faith in you gentlemen of the jury. Her life and future depend on you tonight.' I don't think the jury heeded those words.

"I have saved up a little money I have earned from selling my doilies. I hope to go home to mother. She's getting old and she needs me."

On November 6, 1935, Lyda again applied for a pardon.

"I did not have a fair trail in this unfortunate affair. Through bias, prejudice and propaganda of newspapers and community, the jurors had a set opinion of my case.

"I was tried on first degree murder. The judge instructed the jury to bring in a compromised verdict of second degree manslaughter or acquittal. This was done in order to gain a conviction.

"My aged mother is in a very bad state of health. It is her desire as well as mine to be with her in her declining years."

On May 9, 1940, a letter signed by Twin Falls Police Chief H. U. Gillette and two of Lyda's sisters asked Governor Bottolfsen to give a ten-day reprieve so Lyda could see her ill mother before she died.

Governor Bottolfsen denied the request.

On April Fools' Day, 1941, Mrs. John B. Quigley, Lyda's sister from Nyssa, Oregon, told the Idaho Board of Pardons that Lyda could come live with her and sell her doilies.

But Idaho's new governor was not receptive to the proposal. "It seems to me she has made a practice of taking out insurance on her husbands. I can't vote for her release."

Lyda stayed in prison.

But the new prison reform program had evidently had a definite effect on Lyda Whitlock. She had so ingratiated herself with the warden's wife that she was a member of the domestic staff in the warden's household, sweeping floors and preparing meals. When she was engaged in the latter pursuit, the warden made sure all of the flypaper was accounted for.

Nearly ten years had expired since Lyda had been incarcerated for the second time. Evidently learning the folly of her ways, she had comported herself in a spirit of cooperative decorum. The fact that she had been such a model prisoner through the years had not been lost on the prison parole board.

As a consequence, on October 3, 1941, the state pardon board granted the plump, auburn-haired woman a six-month probationary release, providing she would spend at least the next six months of her life in the home of her sister, Mrs. John Quigley.

Attorney General Bert H. Miller explained to the press that Lyda would be visited frequently by probation officers and would report to the board. At the end of six months, if everything was satisfactory she probably would be given a full pardon.

Not that the government officials were unanimous in their desire to see the legendary Lady Bluebeard released from jail. One condition of the release was that no attempt would be made to exploit her experiences by publication of her story, appearances in vaudeville, or in any other manner.

Clemency for the forty-nine year-old convicted poisoner had been agreed upon by Attorney General Miller and Secretary of State George Curtis. Miller said he voted release because of legal aspects of the case. He claimed Lyda had been charged with poisoning her husband, but convicted of second degree murder although Idaho law required death by poisoning be considered as first degree. There had been evidence of disagreement in the jury, he added.

Secretary Curtis voted for release because, as he put it, "Her debt to society has been paid." Governor Clark had been the lone dissenter, claiming that she menaced society. "I'm afraid of that woman," he commented. "She's a poisoner."

But swaying the board's final decision was its interview of Mrs. Quigley, Lyda's sister, who renewed her offer to give her sister a home and assist her in opening an art shop.

Thus at 2:00 p.m. on October 3, 1941, Melvin La Frenz, working secretary for the board, handed Lyda her release, and within half an hour she was whisked away by Mr. and Mrs. Quigley. Her hair was well coiffured and she wore a well-fitted green dress.

She refused to be interviewed by reporters.

John Quigley was a sugar beet farmer who worked as a night watchman at the sugar mill. He and his wife Blanche lived alone in a two-story wood-framed house in the small potato and sugar beet farming community of Nyssa, in eastern Oregon. Their only daughter, Lurlene Stafford, had grown up and was living with her husband on a farm outside of town.

The word quickly circulated that Lyda was coming to live with her sister in Nyssa. The Sunday after Lyda moved in, the church was packed with twice the number of worshippers who usually attended. But the curious were doomed to disappointment, as Lyda abhorred the way people looked at her and was not a churchgoer anyway. She never attended church that or any other Sunday.

Lyda still had her bubbly personality and a quick smile. She laughed a lot, almost in a childlike way. She still loved animals, and the feeling was mutual. She had names for all the cows on the farm, and it was almost uncanny how they would come to her when she called.

She had a pet parrot that would jump up on her shoulder. When that happened Lyda would laugh so hard the bird would dig its claws in deeper to hang on, and she would laugh even harder. She kept the bird in a large metal cage, but sometimes it would get out and climb the curtains, much to her sister's displeasure. Lyda fell in love with the family cat, and would often be seen stroking its back as it purred contentedly in her lap.

For the six months following the parole, Lyda's behavior was exemplary. She cooperated graciously with the parole board when its members visited her, and she was the personification of the rehabilitated prisoner. Consequently, on April 1, 1943, she was considered no longer a threat to society and was granted a full pardon.

Lyda was now a heavy-set woman who looked much younger than a woman approaching the half-century mark. Her reddish-brown hair was streaked with a touch of gray. Lyda was not lazy; she always did her share of the work around the Quigley household. She was a wonderful cook and a meticulous housekeeper.

Although she never spoke about her former husbands or the life that had made her name synonymous with Bluebeard, she often spoke of how tough prison life had been on her. However, she always had good words to say about the wardens, claiming they had treated her right.

Lyda took a special shine to her niece, Lurlene, whose company she especially seemed to enjoy. Even though Lyda's knees began to suffer from arthritis, causing her to move slowly, she wanted to have her own spending money. So one day in the fall of 1944, Lyda took a job at a potato shed, sorting out bad potatoes. It was a tough job, but Lyda stuck with it all the way through the season. Her ability to drive better than most men occasionally earned her the keys to the family car, and she would take Lurlene's six-year-old daughter downtown to buy an ice cream cone.

People in Nyssa respected the church-going and hardworking Quigleys, and they knew better than to bring up the subject of Lyda's past with the family. Not that they didn't know about it. Neighborhood children soon learned that the new guest at the Quigley home had killed several people. They fancied the house as haunted and would dare each other to run and touch a corner of the porch without getting caught by the murderer.

But Lyda was a happy and docile woman and an ideal guest. She never quarreled with her hosts.

Some two years after she was pardoned, Lyda got a case of the wanderlust. She decided to go home to Twin Falls and live on the family farm, homesteaded by her father. She set up housekeeping in a small worker's house, but soon discovered she was not as welcome here as she had been with her sister Blanche in Nyssa. Her younger sister, Jeanette, near whom she now lived, had attended high school in a building next to the courthouse during the trial. Whole groups of her classmates had attended the hearings. Jeanette, now married, carried resentment for her sister and would rarely visit her.

Lyda also lived next to her older sister, Beulah Sweet, whose husband worked the family farm. Lyda found herself an unwelcome guest there when visitors called. Often, when she was in the main farmhouse when company arrived, Beulah would banish her to an upstairs bedroom.

But there was one person in Twin Falls who did not want to see Lyda stigmatized. She was Ruth Lancaster, a self-proclaimed minister to murderers and career thieves. Considered by natives to be a few bricks short of a load, Ruth had given her old rattletrap of a car a blessing to serve God. When she wasn't visiting prisoners, she would rest her head on its steering wheel and plead for it to go down dusty, abandoned roads to find someone in need of a gospel message. A local newspaper carried the story about Ruth giving Sunday school lessons in jail to Douglas Van Vlack, the man who had distinguished himself by shooting the only county deputy sheriff ever killed in the line of duty. The rest of the town wanted his hide.

Ruth had a morbid curiosity about Lyda, the most infamous criminal she had ever heard about, and set out on a one-woman campaign to save her soul. Ruth finally tracked her down, and was surprised to find her knock on Lyda's screen door one summer day was responded to. Lyda invited her in and welcomed her warmly.

Thus began a series of visits from the evangelist bent on saving Lyda. Ruth convinced her that Lyda was not like the sinners she had met before, many of whom gave off an evil aura. Lyda was not like that at all.

Lyda was grateful for Ruth's weekly visits, which continued throughout her stay in Twin Falls. Unbeknownst to the soul-saver, Lyda was not nearly as interested in the heat of her evangelistic fervor as she was in the warmth of her hands. A hunger for human companionship seemed to be sated as Ruth held Lyda's hands during the hour-long sessions.

One visit, however, seemed to change all of that. Ruth gave Lyda a biblical lesson that struck a deep chord in Lyda. "In the book of John," intoned Ruth, "Jesus is standing by a well when a Samaritan woman approaches him. He tells the woman that the water he gives quenches thirst forever. When the woman asks for this water, Jesus tells her to get her husband. But the woman responds that she has no husband. Jesus then says she answered truthfully, because she has had five husbands, and the man she now lives with is not her husband."

Lyda's eyes widened in astonishment. The story seemed to catch her off guard. An expression of sorrow came into her face as if she were remembering her own husbands. She sank in her rocking chair. "What happened to her husbands?" Lyda asked.

Ruth narrowed her eyes as she studied Lyda's face. The way Lyda had responded suggested she believed the Samaritan woman had killed her former husbands — not a surprising conclusion for Lyda to reach. Instead of responding to Lyda's question, Ruth continued, "the Samaritan woman was converted at the moment she could tell Jesus saw into her past. She went into her village and told everyone what had happened to her."

Lyda's expression changed to one of hope. Tears welled up in her eyes as if she were contemplating salvation. Ruth squeezed the hands of her salvaged sinner and left, secure in the knowledge that she had saved yet another soul.

However, unlike the Samaritan woman with the past Lyda imagined her to have, Lyda preferred to be with people who did not know her past. She soon moved away from her cold sisters to the city of Provo, Utah. Here she used some of her savings to pay the first month's rent on a run-down store that she turned into a handicrafts and secondhand shop.

She finally found the obscurity she had been seeking. But it was not like Lyda to seek obscurity alone.

Hal Shaw was a tall, slender, good-looking man who one day wandered into Lyda's shop. Shaw was a few years younger than Lyda, a distinguished gentleman whose aura of respectability was flawed only slightly by a crippled left hand that he kept in a glove. His increasing appearances at Lyda's store indicated he had time and money to burn.

Although overweight and getting along in years, Lyda still charmed men with her quick smile and good nature. Shaw soon found himself under her spell. A widower with a grown son and daughter, the retired business-man seemed to crave companionship as much as Lyda did.

Several years passed before Lyda saw her siblings again. When she did it was with Hal Shaw, who was now her husband. The two had embarked on a lengthy car trip around the West and had stopped off at Lyda's sisters' and brothers' houses along the way. Shaw, who had gold mining claims near Eureka, Nevada, wore a belt with a large gold nugget embedded in the buckle. He drove a big car and wore expensive clothes. Lyda had lost weight and now wore heavy makeup.

But when Lyda and her husband made their way to Oregon, she confided in her sister Blanche that Shaw's children had found out about her past and didn't like her cooking for their father. Let alone living with him. The children were afraid their father might be a victim of the same fate that had befallen other of Lyda's husbands.

Therefore, it was no surprise to Lyda's family when word got back that a couple of years after Lyda's secret wedding to Shaw, he had disappeared. Lyda assumed that her husband's unannounced and sudden departure had been provoked by his children. She never heard from him again.

Stoically licking her wounds, Lyda quit her secondhand store. She found work in nearby Salt Lake City as a live-in housekeeper. For the last two years of her life she cooked for wealthy bachelors and occasionally waited on tables at neighborhood restaurants.

She was living in the large house of a bachelor, cleaning his house, fixing his meals, and doing his laundry when she began feeling pain in her chest. She went to Dr. K. J. Jenkins, who treated Lyda for symptoms of coronary sclerosis.

Lyda was walking home with a bag of groceries just after darkness fell on February 5, 1958, when the pains returned to her chest. She was only two blocks from home when she dropped the bag of groceries and fell on the sidewalk. A woman in a home across the street saw her and called an ambulance.

Lyda was pronounced dead ten minutes later, at Saint Mark's Hospital. The bachelor Lyda had been working for arranged to have Lyda's body sent by train to Twin Falls.

Although Lyda's family was large, only five relatives came to her services. There was a brief closed viewing Saturday morning at Reynolds Mortuary. Lyda wore a dark dress and her face looked serene.

"She looks nice," Blanche Quigley whispered to her sister.

"We can't let this out," Beulah insisted. "No obituary."

"Someone will eventually see the gravestone and word will get out."

"No they won't. Not if we disguise her name. No one knows her married name or her baptismal name. They won't know it was Lyda."

No one gave a sermon at the informal funeral. After the casket was opened for about fifteen minutes, the undertaker closed the lid.

Interment took place at two o'clock the following morning.

Unverified medical reports supposedly state that Lyda's body was completely hairless at the time of her death. According to Darrell Sweet, Lyda's nephew, it was speculated that while boiling the flypaper to extract the arsenic, Lyda had eventually poisoned herself by inhaling the fumes.

Could it be true that the very weapon she had used to dispatch her victims had contributed to her own comeuppance? Were the words of the folksong about Lyda that is still sung around ghostly campfires based on some kind of truth? That by putting arsenic in her apple pie, Lyda had truly ended up with her just deserts?

Lyda now rests in space Number 3, Section 441 Pinehurst in the Sunset Memorial Park of Twin Falls, Idaho. No one would ever expect that Idaho's notorious Lady Bluebeard occupies the grave with the simple headstone inscribed "Anna E. Shaw." Lyda's name at birth had been Anna Eliza, which was shortened to become Lyda. In an effort to dissuade curiosity-quenchers from visiting the grave of one of the nation's most infamous women, the family resorted to using her childhood name for the headstone.

And thus the curtain is lowered on a most enigmatic woman — the subject of the nation's longest criminal trial up until that time.

There are some who claim that Lyda was innocent, maintaining that she was convicted solely on circumstantial evidence. Others avow that she was a cold, calculating murderer — America's first female serial killer.

The *Twin Falls Daily News* summed it up this way during the trial: "She may be utterly shallow and wholly superficial, an innocent, ignorant victim of a series of extraordinary coincidences; or she may be one of the deepest, cleverest and most cold-blooded women since the days of Lucretia Borgia."

Whichever the case, there is no doubt that Lyda Trueblood-Dooley-McHaffie-Lewis-Meyer-Southard-Whitlock-Shaw was one of the most intriguing characters in the annals of modern crime.

Afterword

Lyda saw several women serve light sentences for murdering people, many of whom were their own husbands. Most were sentenced to manslaughter because it was not considered chivalrous to hang a woman at the time.

Rebecca Chacon shot a man three times after she got in an argument with him at a dance. She served from October 27, 1921, to February 4, 1924.

Marguerite Boggan served from September 24, 1932, to October 4, 1934, for killing her husband at a whorehouse.

Flossie Phillips served five months in 1941 for helping her two brothers tie their father up in the desert and leaving him to die.

Luella Yates killed her neighbor, Leland Draper, during an argument over hogs in 1936. She served a little over fourteen months in prison.

Even Elizabeth L. Lacey, the first woman convicted of first degree murder in Idaho, only served thirteen years and eight months, from 1949 to 1962, after killing two husbands, the first by poison.

Lyda would eventually serve more time than the combined sentences of eleven other women convicted of murder or manslaughter who served with her.

In 1974, Lyda's former home, the Old Idaho Penitentiary, clanged its huge metal doors shut for the last time as a working prison.

It was scheduled to be torn down in that year, the work to be done by the inmates. Fortunately, however, due to the diligence of the Idaho Historical Society, which was spearheaded by a dedicated director named Arthur Hart, the prison was spared by being placed on the National Register of Historic Places.

This fascinating gray stone edifice is now open to the public and has become one of Idaho's most popular visitor attractions. Even Lyda's cell in the women's section of the prison may be visited, having been maintained much like it was during its twenty years of occupation by one of the nation's most notorious and inexplicable women.

And if one visits the grounds during a moonless night, and listens very carefully, one may hear the ghosts of the prison's shuffling inmates. And in the women's ward, above the muted sounds of the summer breeze, one just might hear the sound of a wheezy Victrola playing the stirring strains of "When the Saints Go Marching In."